Time Management

Create Forward Momentum with Time Management

Michael Finlayson

Table of Contents

What is Time Management?

Before I get on to my thoughts about time management, I thought that it would be a good idea to see what others were saying on the subject. And so we start with the inimitable Wikipedia.

"**Time management** is the act or process of planning and exercising conscious control over the amount of time spent on specific activities, especially to increase effectiveness, efficiency or productivity. Time management may be aided by a range of skills, tools, and techniques used to manage time when accomplishing specific tasks, projects and goals complying with a due date. This set encompasses a wide scope of activities, and these include planning, allocating, setting goals, delegation, analysis of time spent, monitoring, organizing, scheduling, and prioritizing. Initially, time management referred to just business or work activities, but eventually the term broadened to include personal activities as well. A time management system is a designed combination of processes, tools, techniques, and methods. Usually time management is a necessity in any project development as it determines the project completion time and scope.

Main Themes of Time Management

The major themes arising from the literature on time management include the following:

- Creating an environment conducive to effectiveness

- Setting of priorities
- Carrying out activity around those priorities
- The related process of reduction of time spent on non-priorities

Time management has been considered to be a subset of different concepts such as:

- Project management. Time Management can be considered to be a project management subset and is more commonly known as project planning and project scheduling. Time Management has also been identified as one of the core functions identified in project management.[1]
- Attention management: Attention Management relates to the management of cognitive resources, and in particular the time that humans allocate their mind (and organize the minds of their employees) to conduct some activities.
- Personal Knowledge management: see below (Personal time management).

Professor Stephen Smith, of BYUI, is among recent sociologists that have shown that the way workers view time is connected to social issues such as the institution of family, gender roles, and the amount of labor by the individual.

Hillary Rettig has identified over-giving to family, friends, work, volunteering or activism, as prime obstacles to managing one's time. She recommends solutions including being aware of one's motives (e.g., striving to be a "hero" or self-sacrificing "saint," or over-giving as a form of procrastination), being clear on your roles and responsibilities, and establishing healthy psychological boundaries.

In recent years, several authors have discussed time management as applied to the issue of digital information overload, in particular, Tim Ferriss with "The 4 hour workweek", and Stefania Lucchetti with "The Principle of Relevance"

Stephen R. Covey has offered a categorization scheme for the time management approaches that he reviewed:

- First generation: reminders based on clocks and watches, but with computer implementation possible; can be used to alert a person when a task is about to be done.
- Second generation: planning and preparation based on a calendar and appointment books; includes setting goals.
- Third generation: planning, prioritizing, controlling (using a personal organizer, other paper-based objects, or computer or PDA-based systems) activities on a daily basis. This approach implies spending some time in clarifying values and priorities.
- Fourth generation: being efficient and proactive using any of the above tools; places goals and roles as the controlling element of the system and favors importance over urgency.

Creating an effective environment

Some time management literature stresses tasks related to the creation of an environment conducive to real effectiveness. These strategies include principles such as:

- Get Organized - paperwork and task triage
- Protect Your Time - insulate, isolate, delegate
- Achieve through Goal management Goal Focus" - motivational emphasis
- Recover from Bad Time Habits" - recovery from underlying psychological problems, e.g. procrastination
- Writers on creating an environment for effectiveness refer to issues such as the benefit of a tidy office or home to unleashing creativity, and the need to protect "prime time". Literature also focuses on overcoming chronic psychological issues such as procrastination.

Excessive and chronic inability to manage time effectively may be a result of Attention Deficit Hyperactivity Disorder (ADHD) or Attention Deficit Disorder (ADD). Diagnostic criteria include a sense of underachievement, difficulty getting organized, trouble getting started, many projects going simultaneously and trouble with follow- through. Some authors focus on the prefrontal which is the most recently evolved part of the brain. It controls the functions of attention span, impulse control, organization, learning from experience and self-monitoring, among others. Some authors argue that changing the way the prefrontal cortex works is possible and offers a solution.

Setting priorities and goals

Time management strategies are often associated with the recommendation to set personal goals. The literature stresses themes such as -

- "Work in <u>Priority</u> Order" - <u>set goals</u> and prioritize
- "Set gravitational goals" - that attract actions automatically

These goals are recorded and may be broken down into a project, an action plan, or a simple task list. For individual tasks or for goals, an importance rating may be established, deadlines may be set, and priorities assigned. This process results in a plan with a task list or a schedule or calendar of activities. Authors may recommend a daily, weekly, monthly or other planning periods associated with different scope of planning or review."

As you can see from this Wikipedia article, time management isn't a particularly complicated subject, it's just that it can be a wee bit difficult.

"If you want to make good use of your time, you've got to know what's most important and then give it all you've got."

Lee Iacocca

You cannot afford to waste your time concentrating on the minutiae. Any task or goal will have key elements to it, and those are the elements that you have to focus on. The minutiae might have to be done at some point, but they are unlikely to be critical to your task. If you fail at your key elements you fail at your task.

"The common man is not concerned by the passage of time, the man of talent is driven by it."

Arthur Schoppenhauer

Not the most politically correct of quotes, but what Schoppenhauer says is worth reading. Most people are indifferent to the passage of time, and despite it being our most precious resource, most people probably don't even think about it.

On the other hand, if you have ambition you will be all too aware of time and its passage. You will have things to do and goals to achieve, so you want and need to make the most out of every moment. If you waste your time then it will take longer to achieve your goals.

"Time = life; therefore, waste your time and waste of your life, or master your time and master your life."

Charles Lakein

Time is our most precious resource and none of us have a finite supply of it. Each second, each minute, each hour that goes by is moment of life that is lost to us forever. Do you make the best of each moment that you have, or do you just let your time drift on by? Whilst we cannot add anything to our life, we can ensure that we make the best use of our time, which in turn means that we have made the best use of our life.

"Make use of time, let not advantage slip."

William Shakespeare

Time is there to be used or abused. We can use it to our best advantage or we can just let it drift past us. How do you regard time?

"Don't be fooled by the calendar. There are only as many days in the year as you make use of. One man gets only a week's value out of a year while another man gets a full year's value out of a week."

Charles Richards

I really like this quote because it shows what you can do when you combine ambition with effective time management skills. Again it come down to your personal choice of whether you let time drift on past you, or whether you use every second of it to your best advantage.

"You can't manage time, time just is."

David Allen

Time management is not about managing time, it's about managing yourself and ensuring that you make the best use of your time. The theory is simple, it's just when you add life into the mix that the problems begin.

"The secret to modern life is finding the measure in time management. I have two kids, career and I travel, and I don't think my life is any different than most couples. The most valuable commodity now for many people is time and how to parcel that out."

Hugh Jackman

He's right. Time management isn't just about how well you perform at work and how you are able to achieve your goals, there's more to it than that! Truly effective Time Management allows you to balance your work life with having a life. If you have a family, a spouse, a partner, friends and family, you need to find time to spend quality time with them. You can't be on the go 24/7 so you need to be able to find the time to relax and chill out. If you don't have a life, then where is the point in relentlessly pursuing your goals?

As I mentioned earlier, time management when you bring it down to basics isn't a particularly complicated subject, it's just that it can be a wee bit difficult.

Time Management

Here are 2 quotes and 1 book title from 3 highly influential authors. Take a moment to think about the words, look at what these authors are telling you, and then apply it to your own life.

"What would you do if you knew you could not fail?"

Anthony Robbins

What would you do? If you knew that you had the ability to create a bright, sparkling future, how what you do it?

"Think and Grow Rich"

Napoleon Hill

Think Rich and Grow Rich is probably one of the greatest developmental books of all time. But why not call it, Work Hard and Grow Rich?

"If you had a heart attack and had to work two hours per day, what would you do? If you had a second heart attack and had to work two hours per week, what would you do?"

Timothy Ferriss

Hopefully you all enjoy good health and will continue to do so. I know from personal experience that you never really think about your health until you lose it. Then everything changes. Can you narrow your focus to concentrate solely on what is important?

These authors are essentially all making the same point, but they're doing so from different perspectives. What they are saying is that our lives are our own and it's up to us how we make the best of them. Whilst your personal circumstances and environment do have some bearing, it's up to you to take action and make the choices that you need to achieve your goals. No one can do it for you, it's your life, you have to take personal responsibility for it and your actions, no one else can do it for you.

I don't think that the vast majority of us never really appreciate what we are capable of doing. These authors have recognized that we all have the power to change our lives by using our latent potential. Tony Robbins knows that lack of self-confidence all too often holds us back. Napoleon Hill called his book Think and Grow Rich because his book is about using the power of our minds to shape our lives. With that analogy, Timothy Ferriss is forcing us to change our thought processes to concentrate solely on what is important, and what is after all just the minutiae.

David Allen, author of **Getting Things Done** and **Ready for Anything,** gets right to the point when he says, "Time is just time, you can't mismanage it. What that really means is that you mismanaged the agreement you had with yourself about what you should have accomplished." I had to think about this one for a moment, but he's right. No one can mismanage time, but we might not make the best use of it. Time can't change how we use it, but we can make the conscious decision to make the most out of our time.

"He then goes on to say that time management is really a complex issue of self-management where work needs to be captured, clarified, organized and reviewed in line with your purpose, values, vision, goals, and strategies. When these things are in line, you'll feel good about how you are managing time. Does that sound complicated?" Why? Is planning your time to ensure that you make the optimum use of what you have really all that difficult? Is it that difficult to focus on what needs to be done in order for you to move forward?

I hope that you now realize that time management is nothing to do with managing time, that's just a convenient label. Time management is how you enable and optimize yourself for success. Time management is your schedule to achieving your personal goals. Time management is how you deal with your internal and external clutter. And I know that I've already said it, but it is worth repeating again, and again, and again. Time management is all about the choices that you have to make to achieve success. You have to make decisions. If you make the right decisions you do well, if you make the wrong ones you don't. Just remember that you are the only one who can make those decisions for you, no one else can.

Clearing out Your Internal Clutter

How many times has time just drifted past without your being aware of what has happened? How many times have you been sat in front of your computer, and yet you have no idea of what you have done? In my case, it's more than a few. There could be a couple of reasons as to why your mind is drifting off. The first is that you might be trying to do too much, and as a consequence you are unable to keep your focus on everything that you need to do, and your mind slows down. Alternatively you might not have prioritized your tasks and you could be spending far too much time working on the minutiae, rather than the important tasks. It doesn't matter who you are, or what you are doing, if you try to do too much you will struggle. If you don't keep your focus on what is important then your mind will drift.

If you want to achieve anything then you have to take responsibility for your own actions. If you have something to do, then do it. If you say that you will do something then do it. Don't find excuses as to why you shouldn't do it, just do it.

Do you have a routine? Once you turn your computer on, what do you do? Do you dive into your emails to see who's contacting you? Do you check your Skype or do you visit all your social media platforms to see what's happening? Do you repeat that routine a number of times during the day?

Whether it's at work or at home we all slip into our routines. Our routines have developed because there are things that it feels natural to do, such as check your emails every time you go to your computer. These routines feel so natural, and so comfortable that they become habits. And the worst thing about some of these habits is that you can end up persuading yourself that you've actually achieved something.

If I may be so bold as to quote Dr. Phil, "How's that been working for you"?

Our nice, safe, secure, comfortable routines tend to be based around the minutiae of our jobs at work, or who we are in life. You need to develop a more time friendly approach to your daily routine. For example, if you need to check your emails, then unless you are waiting for an important one, only check them a couple of times a day, it serves no point to check your inbox multiple times a day. If you're at work then unless you need it, switch your mobile off. If you are trying to work on something important, every time that your attention drifts away to the minutiae you will lose your focus on what is important.

Take some time to work out how much time your routines are costing you, I was shocked when I did! If you can be more effective with your time then you will accomplish more. Try to create new routines that will help you to make the most of your time.

You might be aware that things have to change, but have you done anything about it? You and only you can make the decision to change, and only you can decide that you want to make that change. And if you really do want to change, then when are you going to take action? If not now, then when?

It doesn't matter who you are, it doesn't matter what you do or where you live, if you want to succeed then you have to have the right mindset. You need to take responsibility for your tasks, and you need to hold yourself accountable to yourself for them. You need to commit yourself to do the best possible job, because if you don't then you are just wasting your precious time. Learn to prioritize what you are doing so that you don't waste your time, and so that you get the most out of your time. And don't forget that you have goals that you have to work to, goals that require you to get the job

It doesn't matter who you are, it doesn't matter what you do or where you live, if you want to succeed then you have to have the right mindset. You need to take responsibility for your tasks, and you need to hold yourself accountable to yourself for them. You need to commit yourself to do the best possible job, because if you don't then you are just wasting your precious time. Learn to prioritize what you are doing so that you don't waste your time, and so that you get the most out of your time. And don't forget that you have goals that you have to work to, goals that require you to get the job done.

Procrastination versus Effective Action

If you want to get anything done, if you ever hope to achieve success then you have to take action! It makes sense doesn't it? If you do nothing then you get nothing done, but if you take action you get things done. It doesn't get any simpler than that! But if it's so simple, then why is it so hard to do?

There are some tasks that we can look at and groan. It could be that they are boring, it could be that they are difficult, or they could be those fun, wonderful tasks that you want to avoid like the plague. The problem is that if you have something to do, you just can't bury your head in the sand and hope that it goes away, it has to be done at some point. Regardless of how much you loathe the task, you need to deal with it before it becomes an urgent task.

Procrastination can bring you grinding to a halt, it wastes your precious time and it makes it much more difficult for you to achieve your goals. The longer that you procrastinate your tasks the more difficult it will be for you to complete them. The more comfortable your mind becomes with procrastination, the less likely you are to pursue your goals. Your mind will be content to take the east route, and you cannot afford to let that happen!

You cannot afford to let you mind become accustomed to inactivity and lack of drive! It is vital that you deal with procrastination before it has a chance to get settled in.

Here Are a Selection of Procrastination Busting Tips:

i. Take a moment to look at your thoughts. If your mind has too much negativity sloshing around it then you have problems. If you want to achieve, then you have to push yourself forward, and you have to operate outside of your comfort zone. It takes a lot less effort to give up on your goals that it does to pursue them. If your mind is full of negativity then it will whisper into your ear words of defeat, it will tell you that you will never succeed, that you can't do it, and that it's okay to give in, and if you are not careful you will start to listen to it.

In order to beat the negativity you have to reprogram your mind to think more positively. Look in a mirror at least once a day and tell yourself that you are great 5 times, and when you say it, mean it! Write down the positives about yourself, and when you are feeling negative remind yourself of just how good you are. It might take time, but every positive affirmation that you utter will help to change your negative thinking into a more positive frame of mind. Repetition is the key to success. The more that you tell yourself that you are great the more you will come to believe it.

ii. When is the best time of the day for you to get work done? We've all got times where we are able to work more effectively than others. For some bizarre reason my optimum times are far too early in the morning, and after 9pm. For whatever reason I can always accomplish far more at those times than at any other point in the day. So if you have problem tasks, then save them for your optimal work time. Although please don't forget that if your problem tasks are urgent, you're just going to have to grit your teeth and get on with them. It's always worth remembering that no matter how repugnant the task, completing it will get you one step closer to your goals.

iii. You have to prioritize and make a list. You will never get anything done if you don't plan your workload. If you have something to do then plan how you will achieve it. Break the task down into its constituent parts and plan how you will deal with them. Prioritize everything! There is no point in your getting caught up in the minutiae and ignoring the important tasks. Your focus has to be on dealing with the most important tasks first! If you don't complete your important tasks then you will not achieve your objectives.

I used to take each day as it came, and I'm sad to say that I wasn't particularly organized in how I approached my days. One day one of my old managers, in no uncertain terms pointed out the wisdom of a daily, to do list, and from that point on things changed. Put on your list what you need to achieve for the day. Don't get carried away, just go for what you know that you can realistically achieve. Now that you have your day planned you can pursue your tasks in order of importance. At the end of the day, look at what you have achieved. Did you manage to complete your list and if not, why not? It may be a simple thing to do, but creating a daily, things to do list will really focus your mind on how you spend your time.

iv. Remember that you are only human and that there is only so much in the day that you can accomplish. Trying to do too much won't make you a better worker, it can stretch you to breaking point, it can damage your efficiency and productivity, and it could cost you your goals.

If you are trying to do too much then you might end up missing your deadline, you might make a mess of your tasks, or you might not complete them. Are you overextending yourself? You need to learn to say no! I can understand why you might want to overextend yourself, but it won't do you or the quality of your work any good. I realize that saying no to your boss might not be a good career move, but where you are able, explain the situation as to why you can't take any extra work on. Please remember that if you are trying to do too much, then you will not be able to give your key tasks the focus that they need, and your productivity levels will drop.

v. Don't you just love those distractions that beset or daily lives and how they eat up our time. Checking your emails, texts, messages, and social media platforms can eat up a hideous amount of time! Unless you are expecting something important then you just need to check your messages a couple of times a day. If you are trying to get something done, could I suggest that you stay well clear of the social media platforms! And what about everyone who has a question that only you can answer. Fair enough if it's only a couple of people, but the more people who need to eat your time up, the less you will achieve. Be diplomatic about it, but have some kind of do not disturb signal that warns everyone are busy and not

24

to approach you. Never forget that if you are working on important tasks then they take precedence.

vi. Become a decision maker and not a ditherer. You need to take some time to plan out your projects and tasks before you get started, because if you don't know what you are supposed to be doing, then you will struggle. Once you have started and you know what you are doing, then you have to be able to make swift, sharp decisions. You have enough to do without spending an age contemplating your next move.

If you spend an age thinking about your next move, then you can end up talking yourself out of taking any action. If you have difficulties in taking action, if you have problems in making decisions, then there is a simple trick you can use to train your mind. Use a stopwatch and give yourself a maximum of one minute to make your decision before you move on. You can download on online stopwatch there are plenty to choose from.

vii. You're human and not an automaton. You cannot keep going on and on indefinitely and expect to maintain peak performance unless you motivate yourself. Achieving your goals is a great motivator, but that could take a long time so what about the interim period? If you find ways to reward yourself along the way then your journey will go a lot more smoothly. Given that there will always be tasks that are difficult, and tasks that you loathe, set yourself a reward for each one that you complete. Give yourself targets to achieve and reward yourself for achieving them. Rewards always motivate, so take advantage of that.

viii. Use your mind. Take a moment to think about the time that you spend away from your computer. For example when you're driving too and from work, when you're buying your groceries, when you're working in the garden, all those times when your mind is not actively engaged in anything. When your mind is not productively engaged it can start to worry, it can start to think negative thoughts, and you need to deal with that!

Being able to displace negative thoughts for positive ones is a massive help, but there is a simple trick that can also help you in your job. Carry a notebook or even just a scrap of paper with you. Think on how you can improve what you do, or maybe you could make some tweaks to your project, and then write them down. How many times have you had a really great idea then forgotten about it? Once you have written it down then your mind will become more focused on it. It's a simple trick and it works for me in keeping my mind clear of negativity.

ix. Set yourself realistic goals, it's the sensible thing to do, but you shouldn't like sensibility stop you from reaching for the stars! You could look at a project in its entirety and become overwhelmed by the immensity of it all, it can be all too easy to talk yourself into inaction. Once you believe that you are unable to achieve something, it can be very difficult to change that belief. This holds true for whatever you hope to achieve be it work or in your life.

The easiest way to deal with your goals, tasks, or projects is to break then down into simple manageable steps. You will find it much easier working from step to step, rather than approaching your goal in its entirety. Working to achievable steps is much less overwhelming than working to a distant goal. When you are doing something achievable your mind won't try to convince you that you'll never do it. And if your mind is happy then you will be a lot more positive in your ability to achieve your goal.

x. If you have tasks that you are finding particularly difficult or unpleasant, then you could end up wasting a lot of time on them, because it's difficult to give those kinds of tasks the attention that they need. One way to deal with this is to work at those tasks in time blocks. Personally I would set your timer for a maximum of 30 minutes, during this time you need to work as intensely as you can on your task. Once the timer hits 0 then take a break, go work on something else, and then return to your task feeling refreshed and ready for another timed block. If you do it this way then whilst your tasks might not become any more pleasant, you'll be able to work through them a lot more quickly.

Drivers that Destroy Forward Momentum

In my research for this book I have come across the concept of drivers. Not horseless carriage drivers, but psychological drivers. What are these drivers? They are based upon the work of Dr. Taibi Khaler and his theory of Process Communication. These aren't things that we consciously think about, but they are what we do to try and gain the recognition that we need from our peer group.

The drivers are:
Be Perfect
Hurry Up
Try Hard
Please Others
Be Strong

All of us have some of these drivers present in ourselves to a lesser or greater extent. On the face of it these drivers seem really quite positive qualities to have. They give the impression that they are encouraging dedication and motivation, or do they?

However, all is not as it appears on the surface. When you start digging in to what the drivers represent, you will find that they can have a negative impact on what you are trying to achieve. They do nothing to foster any semblance of ambition, and if anything they can do significant damage to our self-esteem.

However, all is not lost. However, before you do anything, you have to recognize that these drivers are causing you a problem, and you have to be prepared to take action to deal with them. Once you can identify the drivers, you can deal with them through positive affirmations and talking them down.

Be Perfect Driver

If you want to achieve you should always want to do your best and to keep pushing yourself forward. However, wanting to do your best is one thing, trying to be perfect is something completely different.

Now I'm too old and set in my ways to really care if I'm ever going to be perfect or not, for which I give thanks. Unfortunately our society places far too much value on the mythical concept of perfection. In one respect you can't blame people who strive for perfection, because wherever you turn the media ceaselessly bombards us with images of perfection. And if you take notice of those images often enough, then you will come to believe that perfection is something to be desired.

We all have things that we are good at and things that we really shouldn't try. The problem for those burdened with the Be Perfect Driver, is that if they don't do everything perfectly, then they will take it to heart and that could have an impact on their self-esteem.

The Be Perfect Driver can limit what work you take on, to only that which you know that you can be perfect at. Consequently you will never achieve what you are capable off.

Being unable to achieve the perfection that you need, can be seriously debilitating, after all, if you can't achieve perfection then why should you bother? When you stop caring then you lose your drive and ambition. When you no longer care then you are at risk of abusing your body through overeating, alcohol and drugs.

The first step in dealing with the Be Perfect Driver, as it is with all the drivers is to admit that you have a problem, and then you have to decide that you want to deal with it, because nobody else can. You have to recognize that no one is perfect.

One way hammering home the lesson that no one is perfect is to research the lives of successful people.

Just like all of us, successful people have made mistakes, it's just that they don't treat them as mistakes, think more along the lines of, "so that didn't work, now how about this." So see where they went wrong, and see what they have achieved in their lives.

You have to talk to yourself, you have to tell yourself that, "It's okay to be less-than-perfect, it's okay to be human, and it's okay to make mistakes." It will take some time, but once you condition your mind to think more positively, it will think more positively!

Be Strong Driver

To achieve anything in life you have to make some tough decisions, you have to be able to step out of your comfort zone, and you have to be able to deal with anything that life throws at you. And yes you could say that this means that you have to be strong. However, in the context of the drivers, being strong takes on a meaning that could prove to be detrimental to your health, and your hopes of achieving your goals.

To achieve anything in life you have to make some tough decisions, you have to be able to step out of your comfort zone, and you have to be able to deal with anything that life throws at you. And yes you could say that this means that you have to be strong, but in this context, being strong takes on another meaning.

The Be Strong Driver requires you to set aside your feelings, your wants and needs, because to give in to them is a sign of weakness. With this driver you have to hide your feelings away, as any show of weakness is unacceptable. This is a driver that can have its roots in childhood, when vulnerability could leave a child prone to ridicule. And sadly as those children grow up, they carry the Be Strong Driver with them.

This driver requires you to do everything yourself. No matter how heavy your workload you will shy away from asking for help. This driver can have a massive negative effect on your productivity levels and efficiency.

The way to deal with this driver is to accept that you have a problem, and recognize that you want to change it. Tell yourself that it's okay to have feelings, feelings aren't a sign of weakness they are a sign of strength. Tell yourself that it's okay to ask for help, that it's okay to express your feelings. By bottling up your feelings you will not only be unable to move forward, but you will be creating a time bomb for yourself. I should state that the only feelings that should never be expressed is violence.

Hurry Up Driver

If you have a job then you need to just get on with it and finish it. The sooner that you complete it the sooner you can move on to your next task. Obviously that's what happens in an ideal world. In the real world we have the joys of procrastination, and the obstacles that life so loves to send us.

As you can probably guess, the Hurry Up Driver wants you to do more and more as quickly as possible. This is a driver that makes us impatient with ourselves and with others. There is no better example of this than drivers on the road who are impatient with delays, and have to travel as quickly as possible in order to shave a couple of minutes off their journey time.

By constantly pushing yourself it is inevitable that you will makes mistakes. By taking on every scrap of work that you can, everyone might be impressed by your energy and dedication. And that warm glow of approval will stay with you, right up to the point when they see the quality of your work.

You cannot rush a job and expect it to be done to the highest standard. If you rush then not doing the job properly will affect your productivity. In order to maintain competitiveness most companies have to work to strict deadlines. If you do a rush job then the quality of your work might not be acceptable, or the mistakes that you make might mean that you miss the deadline.

I'm sad to say that this type of driver is on the increase. It could be that it is a symptom of our consumer driven society where we demand instant gratification. But for whatever the reason, there are far too many people who are always in a constant hurry. It's a habit that might have become so ingrained, that those who are affected by it probably don't even realize it.

It's sad that not enough people seem to want to take a step back and think about what they are doing. People are more content to rush without thought, rather than spend the time to think on how they might best use their time.

As with all the other drivers you need to accept that you have a problem, and recognize that you want to deal with it. You have to recognize that by going too quickly, you can end up making rash, impulsive, inept decisions that will at some point come back to haunt you.

You need to realize that the most effective course of action is one that has been properly thought out, and planned to the point where all foreseeable eventualities and prepared for.

Please Others Driver

It's a good thing to have the respect and approval of your peers. It's good for your self-esteem and self-belief. It means that you know that you're doing the right thing and that your peers respect you for it. Having the respect of your peers is not essential for your success, but it does give you a significant psychological boost.

Those who are subject to the demands of the Please Others Driver are desperate for approval. This desperation for approval leads sufferers of this driver to feel anxiety, depression, and to continually live in fear of rejection, even by those who are not important to them. If you have even a trace of this driver in you I would strongly suggest that you deal with it!

Sufferers struggle to assert their own needs. Not being able to assert their individual needs can lead to resentment which is bottled up until there is an incident. This kind of driver can result in promising the earth in order to win approval, and then being unable to keep that commitment.

You need to accept that you have a problem, and you have to want to deal with it. You have to be able to understand that there is a measure of give and take in all relationships. You need to accept the fact that there is nothing wrong with thinking about yourself and acting in your best interests, it doesn't mean that you're being selfish, it's a sign of self-respect. By making the decision to act in your best interests, it means that your primary focus is no longer on pleasing others. Should you decide to please others then it should be because you choose to, and not because you feel that you are obliged to.

Try Hard Driver

The Try Hard Driver is nothing to do with just working hard and doing your best, it's a lot more than that. In the ordinary run of things you know when enough is enough. You know that there are times when you need to take a break, and you know when you have taken on enough work to keep you busy.

Those who have the Try Hard Driver are unable to set limits on what they do. Whilst they are very enthusiastic on tackling any task laid before them, they are more committed to trying to do the job rather than actually getting it done. There's more to getting a job done than just being enthusiastic! Being able to complete your job on time and to the best of your ability is more important than enthusiasm. Try hard Drivers seem to be unaware that they can't do everything and that there is only so much time in the day.

If you are unable to admit that you have a problem, and that you need to deal with it, then you will be stuck with it. With this driver the way to deal with it is to learn to say **NO!**

The world won't come to an end if you don't overextend yourself. You don't have to sit on a multitude of committee's and volunteer to take on every project that is offered to you. You have to learn to understand your own limitations and you have to make sure that everyone else knows what they are. You don't have to do everything yourself, you can get help. And most important of all, learn to relax!

Not everyone has every driver, we tend to have a mixture that is unique to us. We are stronger in some drivers and weaker in others. I concede that the drivers do have their positive points, but I think that the weaknesses far outweigh the positives. Paradoxically we believe that our drivers can actually help us, when in reality they are much more a hindrance than a help.

You can learn to deal with your drivers by learning to turn a positive to a negative. Keep repeating your positive affirmations on a daily basis, regardless of whether you are at work or at home. By working on your positive affirmations you are essentially reprogramming your mind, and you will not achieve that overnight.

Dealing with your drivers will take time, because anything that requires changing the habits of a lifetime does take time. It will take effort, and it will require you to take action because if you don't take action you will achieve nothing. Once you bring your drivers under control you can improve your productivity and efficiency, and most important of all, you can resume the active pursuit of your goals.

Learning to Focus

I don't know if you have ever read Timothy Ferriss's book, The Four Hour Work Week? Inside it he has a chapter on Time Management in which he tells us to forget all about it. He asks us 5 very searching questions:

1. If you had a heart attack and had to work two hours per day, what would you do?

2. If you have a second heart attack and had to work two hours per week, what would you do?

3. If you have a gun to your head and had to stop doing 4/5ths of different time-consuming activities, what would you remove?

4. What are the top three activities that I use to fill time to feel as though I've been productive?

5. Learn to ask, "If this is the only thing I accomplished today, will I be satisfied with my day?"

Whilst Ferriss might not have the most conventional views on Time Management, no one can doubt his great respect for focus! These questions are designed to get us to focus on the important things, and to minimize or to completely get rid of the minutiae. And it makes good sense! You will never get anything done if you focus on the minutiae rather than your important tasks. You might not be able to dispose of all the minutiae, but if you try to dispose of some of the important things then you will fail. If you've not already done it, how would you answer those 5 questions?

Another thing that Ferriss also talks about is the Pareto principle. The Pareto Principle, also known as the 80-20 rule states that, "roughly 80% of the effects come from 20% of the causes." For example in business 80% of your profits come from 20% of your customers. The more efficient you are, the more your refine what you do, the more that you target your customers, the more efficient you are with time, the more you will achieve.

Ferriss also talks about Parkinson's law. Parkinson's law was promulgated by Cyril Parkinson and it is based on his experiences with the U.K Civil Service. His initial observations came about through his observations on the expansion of bureaucracies. And as I'm sure that you'll agree, there is nothing quite like a bureaucracy to demonstrate the principles of expansion.

In relation to time management it states that a task will swell in importance and complexity in relation to the time allotted for its completion. Ferriss quite rightly contends that in giving too much time to any task, we will over complicate it.

However, we will achieve more, and complete our work to a higher standard, if we devote less, but more targeted time to it. Work smarter not harder. This is all about the need for focus. If you have too much time, then you don't have the same focus that you would with a tight deadline. So look at how you spend your time. Are you focused on getting your task done, or do you just wander along in your own time.

Here's a useful, quick exercise for you to examine your focus. As with all the exercises that I set you, I want you to be brutally honest with yourself, otherwise you won't gain the understanding that you need. What is your 20%? How much time do you spend doing the 80% in order to avoid doing the 20%? If you can answer yourself honestly, then the chances are that you understand what focus is. Follow these steps to achieve your focus:

i. You need to decide what your 20% is, and this will probably vary from project to project.

ii. Once you have your 20% you need to work out why you are not focusing on it.

iii. Once you know what you have to do, work out how you're going to do it, then do it.

Far too many of us waste far too much time in pursuing the minutiae. These tend to be the trivial, unimportant tasks, but completing them makes us feel good because we convince ourselves that we are actually achieving something. However, if your focus is predominantly on the minutiae then you are unlikely to accomplish anything. In order to achieve in life or at work, it is vital that you remain laser focused on what is most important to you at work and in your life.

Please remember that no one can make you focus on anything. It's up to you to take action and make the conscious decision that you can do it and that you will do it.

You Need a Plan

If you have ever taken the time to study how successful people succeed you will come across a common trend. This commonality is nothing special, in fact it's something for which we all have the potential. It comes as no great surprise to learn that successful people work hard to achieve their goals. It's a fact of life that you have to put the time in, in order to build the foundation for your success. But then there are a lot of people who work hard, and they are still trying to achieve that elusive thing called success. That's because it's not about just working hard, it's also about working smarter.

People who have achieved success tend to share certain traits. Those who have worked their way up to the top ranks of society certainly possess these traits. They are:

i.   The power of persistence
ii. The power of passion
iii. The power of self-control
iv. The power decision and action
v.   The power of creativity

The Power of Persistence

Just because someone is successful it doesn't mean that they have not experienced failure. A great example is Thomas Edison who experienced over a thousand failures before inventing the electric light bulb. How about Henry Ford, a man who came from nothing but who revolutionized production. You might recall a certain someone who failed in business and failed in running for office, he ended up as President of the U.S, and his name was Abraham Lincoln.

Successful people don't regard failure as the end of the world. It might be an inconvenience but it's also a learning experience. When you know what doesn't work you continue to work to find something that does. Once you find what works then you pursue it and use it to your best advantage.

You could be the luckiest person on the face of the earth. You could set the standard for intelligence. You could be an idea's person that could change the world. But unless you have persistence, unless you can keep moving forward no matter what, then do you really believe that you can achieve what you are capable off? No matter how well you plan things through, life will continually throw obstacles at you. Those who succeed will deal with those obstacles, they will learn what they can from them, and they will move on. Far too many of us give up too soon We tell ourselves that we can't do something and we walk away from it.

You will never succeed if you walk away. There may be times when no matter what you do it's not going to work, so then you have to be realistic. But if you walk away from something that you still have a chance of succeeding with, then you will damage your confidence, and you will show your mind that it okay to give in.

I wonder how many people have walked away from something just when they were on the cusp of success. No matter how difficult things are, you have to try. As long as you keep trying you will believe in yourself, you will have faith in your ability to succeed, but the moment that you stop...

I have a couple of quotes for you from Winston Churchill. He was someone who faced seemingly impossible odds. It would have been all too easy to say I give in. Regardless of who you are, being the one who has to make the decisions can be a very lonely place.

"If you're going through hell, keep going."

Winston Churchill

"Never, never, never, never give up."

Winston Churchill

Two quotes that total 13 words. As you can see, when you put them together in the right order you have 13 words that can take your through anything. Here are the success traits that you need in order to achieve success.

The Power of Passion

When you're in the upper echelons of sport, politics, business, entertainment, science research and every other field where you pit yourself against an adversary, winning is important. Even more so when you consider that losing or poor performance could have financial implications.

Let's say that there's a rugby game and one side is losing big time. It's half time, the winning team walk off the pitch supremely confident that they're going to win. But as we all know in life, nothing is ever certain. Once the second half began the victors of the first side lost their way, they had become complacent and had lost their focus. At half time, the team manager of the losing team had words with them, he fired them up, he re-ignited their passion and they went out and ground their opposition into the dust.

Have you ever heard the expression," if you can believe it, you can achieve it." Essentially it means that if you have something that you need to bring to fruition, just going out and doing it is not enough. If you have goals that you want to achieve then you have to have passion. You have to have to believe that you can achieve your goals, and you have to have a burning desire to want to achieve them.

Two examples that should motivate you are Sir Richard Branson and Lord Sugar. They built their empires from nothing. They faced problems along the way, they made mistakes, but that didn't stop them because they believed, and they had passion for what they were doing.

Passion gives you the drive and determination to achieve your goals regardless of whatever difficulties that you meet along the way. You may believe that you are not that kind of person, personally I disagree. You can find the spark of passion in you and you can develop it, but you have to want to do it!

The Power of Self-Control

Your power of self-control can either make you or break you. The power of self-control is how you handle your thoughts and emotions, which in a business setting is crucial.

Let's say for example that you're trying to sign up a new client. You could be feeling very nervous as this client could mean a lot for your organization if you get them, and even more for you if you don't. Regardless of how you are feeling you have to come across as cool and collected, the consummate professional.

Our thoughts and emotions could have us focused on productivity and deliverability, but they could also have us languishing in procrastination. Your ability to take action, to focus, to create forward momentum, and to deal with any drivers that are causing you problems, is what will drive you forward and help you to succeed.

The Power of Decision and Action

Studies have found that one of the greatest causes of failure is the inability of an individual to make decisions. Allied with that we have procrastination, which is the most common factor that prevents people from achieving their full potential. It's been shown that those at the top of their game are able to make decisions promptly.

If you can't make decisions then you will be unable to take action, which means that you will achieve nothing. If you are unable to make prompt decisions then you will delay whatever you are working on, and that is likely to have financial implications. If you rush into making poorly thought out decisions, then they can have a significant impact on you and your business.

Decision making requires you to be in possession of all the relevant facts. Unless you are in possession of all the relevant facts, then you cannot make any pertinent decisions. You might have to rely on others to help source the information that you need, it might take longer than you are happy with, but who cares, it doesn't matter! You cannot take effective, productive action unless you are in full possession of the facts.

Once you have all your information, then formulate a plan and take action. Be aware that your situation can change, so keep your information fresh, and make any changes as and when necessary.

The Power of Creativity

The really great success stories start with one single, solitary, good idea. Impossible problems are solved with one idea. One idea can win you new business. One idea can transform your companies KLT factor. One idea can make you stand out from the crowd. One idea can completely turn your business around.

Sometimes you can stick with what has worked, but sometimes you have to not just step outside of the box, you have to leap out of it.

If you are struggling to come up with fresh ideas, then look at what has worked previously. But if you have to depend on what others have done before you, then that might not work for you or your current situation.

You don't have to look for grand, ferociously complicated solutions, not when the simple alternative can be the most effective. If a solution is not readily apparent then create one. Whatever you do, never let your mind be bound up by convention because that will destroy your creativity. Be bold, be different, and remember that no matter how outlandish your idea, it could be the one that moves you and your business forward.

When you put together a personal plan of action, you should bear in mind the success traits, and you should look to incorporate them into everything that you do. The more that you work with the success traits the more natural they will become to you.

This chapter concludes our clear out of your mental clutter, and it should have you on the path to a positive mindset. The next stage is to clear out the clutter from your working life.

Clearing the Clutter in Your Business

How organized are you? Do you plan? Do you prioritize? Do you use a list? Or do you close your eyes and hope for the best?

In this chapter I am going to focus on confronting and dealing with the external clutter. Your external clutter is the mess that is created when you work with inefficient systems or no systems at all. It's nice to be able to do what you want, when you want, and if it works for you in your spare time then fine, but don't go to work with that kind of attitude! If you have that kind of attitude at work then it will impact on your productivity and efficiency.

It doesn't take a lot to get rid of your external clutter you just need to make some simple changes in the way that you work.

i. Prioritize Your Tasks

Different people have different ways of prioritizing their tasks Some prefer to deal with their most difficult tasks in the morning, when they are at their most alert. Doing it this way means that you feel like you've achieved something, which makes the rest of your day feel more relaxed. Others like to create momentum by starting with the easier tasks first. You have to find your own way, but personally I keep my focus on completing my most important tasks first.

In whatever job you have, you will have tasks that are important for the success of whatever you are involved in. You will also have tasks that are less important, and less urgent. It is vital for your success that you deal with your important tasks first. If you spend too much time working on your less important tasks, then your productivity levels could suffer, and you might not meet your deadlines.

ii. Plan Your Time

In order to be effective in what you do you need to plan your time. You need to know what you are doing and when you are doing it. Without knowing what you are doing then how can you structure your day, how can you organize yourself? Without planning your time, it will be difficult to prioritize your tasks. You will in effect be a loose cannon that crashes about in all directions.

Depending on your role depends to what level you plan. You might even have someone who plans your schedule for you. Even if you have everything meticulously planned in some grand timetable, you still need a daily to do list.

Either the night before, or before you head in to work, write down what you need to accomplish for the day. The aesthetics of your list are immaterial and you can use any old scrap of paper for it. What is important about your to do is that it has caused you to focus on what you need to achieve. You are only human, and with the best will in the world there is no guarantee that you will remember everything, so write it down.

At the end of your day, review what you managed to achieve. Were you able to achieve everything that was on your to do list? If you weren't then why couldn't you? And what can you do to stop a recurrence of that situation.

By thinking on the day ahead, and on the day that's done, you will start to think more on what you do. When you are more focused on your performance and your efficiency then your productivity will improve. If it works for me then it can work for you.

Don't try to overcomplicate your planning! When you complicate things you are much less likely to follow through on them, and a complicated plan is much more prone to things going wrong.

Have all of your important dates on a calendar, or whatever system you use. If you are working on a project then you need to know what needs to be done, and by when. For your daily tasks a simple to do list is more than sufficient. Planning your time will always enhance your time management.

iii. Limit your distractions

You have more than enough to contend with at work. The last thing that you want to do is to waste precious time with distractions. Which of you has been brave enough to cut down on your distractions? How many of you have fallen prey to the lure of the social media platforms. How many of you can't bear not to repeatedly check your emails throughout the day. And how many of you, when you're feeling a wee bit bored don't start playing computer games.

The art of communication is a wonderful thing, but it can be a major irritant if people keep talking to you when you're trying to work.

Most of us don't work well when there are constant distractions. They make it impossible to focus, they irritate us, and they eat up our time. Unfortunately this is something that you have to deal with yourself.

Your success will require willpower on your part, as many of your distractions have become ingrained habits that you need to break. And don't forget that just because it might be difficult, it doesn't mean that it's impossible.

Unless you're expecting something important then only check your emails a couple of times a day. If you don't want your work colleagues to disturb you then let them know, haul up a **DO NOT DISTURB** flag.

If you have calls to make then set yourself a time limit on your calls. That should focus you to be more precise and keep to the subject of your call.

It can be difficult dealing with distractions that you enjoy. One thing that you can do is just switch them all off. Now that might be stressful, so give yourself a reward once you've completed your tasks.

Record how much time you waste with all your distractions. And once you've seen the hideous amount of time that you lose, monitor how much work you get done with your distractions switched off, as compared to when they are on. The results just might surprise you.

iv. Set a Specific Time to Work on the Minutiae

Less important tasks can be annoying distractions that can hold you back from achieving your goals. However, just because just because they take you away from your main tasks, it doesn't mean that you don't have to complete them.

Like anything in life, how you deal with them very much depends on who you are. If you are disciplined in your approach, then you can spread out such dynamic activities as checking your emails and making phone calls, throughout your day.

If you spend long periods on the phone because you enjoy making your calls, and doing so does nothing for your productivity, then you are wasting time that could be better used elsewhere. So only make your calls after you have concluded your important tasks for the day, and put a time limit on them. By timing your telephone calls you will get into the habit of keeping your calls laser focused, which will probably be appreciated by whatever busy individual that you are calling. More targeted call should result in an increase in your productivity.

Emails are a fantastic communication tool, but checking your inbox on a regular basis will drain your time away. Your emails are like bright, shiny objects that you feel compelled to look at, despite the fact that the majority of them are likely to be junk, you can find yourself opening every one, just in case you miss anything. You want to time just how long you spend trawling through your emails on an average day, it might shock you.

If emails are a weakness of yours, then unless you are expecting anything important, leave them until you have completed your important tasks. Set yourself a time for going through your emails. It might be difficult at first, but it will help you to sort your important emails from the trash.

If you are someone who works from home, then you have even more distractions to cope with. Without a manager looking over your shoulder you need to be exceptionally disciplined, otherwise you could take far too many extended breaks. If you have clients that you deal with, then you need to make sure that they know when they can and can't call, such as during family time or evening meals. Having the background noise from family life is not conducive to clear thinking, and it's not the kind of thing that your clients want to hear.

v. **Automate Your Tasks**

Your time is the most valuable thing that you possess. Once your day has gone, it's gone and you will never see it again. Have you certain tasks that you repeat again and again, then it's worth looking at ways to automate them. If you can automate certain tasks then that could free up a lot of time.

Technology might want to make you bang your head against a wall, but it's also a fantastic way to automate tasks. If you have to send multiple, similar out then use an autoresponder. If you need to use multiple passwords throughout your day, then use software to remember them. If you write then you can use voice recognition software such as Dragon Naturally Speaking, to do it for you. If you have to send multiple emails of a similar type out, then use templates.

If you have tasks that you repeat again, and again and again, then why not look to see if technology can help you. If you are looking to organize your notes then Evernote will help. If you're organizing on a grander scale, for example planning a project, then Basecamp project management can help. Do you have problems, and do you waste time trying to deal with all of your passwords, then why not take a look at Roboform Password Protection. If you need to hold meetings, presentations, conferences or deliver training, it can be a huge expense in time and money to bring everyone together. Webinars can bring together people from all around the world, and GVO Conference is probably the best that I've come across.

Just don't get so carried away with all the available technology that you forget to use your mind. Make sure that any technology you invest in does make things easier for you, because technology can also complicate things for you.

vi. Organize Your Online & Offline Files

Depending on the state that your files are in, this can be a particularly daunting task for which I have the utmost sympathy for you, but it's worth it! I once had the joy of organizing a retail organization's paper sales orders, and that was such fun. Once you have your files organized then you can save yourself a lot of time and misery hunting for necessary information.

Personally I think that getting your computer files into order is one of the most time saving things that you can ever do, especially if you're storing terabytes of information.

If your workstation and computer is brimming over with information and files then it can seem to be an impossible task, but not if you break it down into manageable chunks. You don't have to do it all at once, just do it a bit at a time. Once all your files are in order you will instantly be able to find the information that you need, which means that you won't have any delays in completing your tasks for the day.

vii. Use Headphones to Block out Noise

Okay, so this might sound a strange thing to say, but I have a talent for things like that. We all know that if you are trying to work in a noisy environment then you are going to have an extremely difficult job in trying to maintain your focus and concentration. If you can't stay focused then your work rate will drop. One simple way to deal with this is through the use of noise cancelling headphones or earplugs. Once you can diminish your background noises, you should be able to focus on what is important.

viii. Get a Comfortable Chair and Some Good Lighting

It's quite possible that you have been uncomfortable for such a long period of time that you no longer notice it. You are not going to be at your most productive if you are sitting in an uncomfortable chair, or if you have indifferent lighting. I realize that it might seem like a trivial point, but your personal comfort can have a significant impact on your productivity levels. It can make a noticeable difference in how you feel, and if you are no longer in any discomfort, then it follows that your productivity will rise.

ix. Clean up Your Workspace

And yes I do realize that this is an obvious thing to say, but have you noticed how many people have a less than organized workspace? If you spend your day surrounded by a junkyard then it can have a negative effect on you, just as rummaging through stacks of paper to find what you need, can be intensely frustrating. If you have a clean, neat, organized desk then it is much easier to remain focused. You only have to get your desk organized once in order to keep it clean, logical, and much more user friendly. It might take a bit of time but it will be worth it.

Your Business Inventory

We all have different tools and gadgets that we use, and we have different routes to achieving our objectives. I want you to take a long, hard look at everything that you do and use.

For this exercise I want you to judge the worth of your activities and tools based on their financial cost, and their cost in time. If there is something that you do or use, or if it's not giving you an acceptable ROI then you need to get rid of it. You need to identify everything that's making you inefficient, and deal with it, so make a realistic assessment if your systems or tools fall into the profit or loss bracket.

These questions will help you to determine what changes if any that you should make:

i. Out of everything that you do, what's working well for you?

ii. What activity or expenditure brings you no profit, and what takes more time than it's worth?

iii. What you should keep and why?

iv. What you should get rid of and why?

Come up with categories for your tasks and expenditure. Now as we all do different things, then we will all have different categories. To make it easier to organize you might want to put it all on a spreadsheet. To give you an idea, these are my categories:

i. Research
ii. Writing
iii. Blogs
iv. Marketing
v. Forum memberships
vi. FaceBook groups
vii. Training
viii. Any other item that costs you time or money
ix. Any item that is parked with no activity and not making money

Your inventory should help you to achieve two main goals. The first is that it will give you an understanding of what you do with your time and money, and it should also focus your mind on how to make the best use of what you have. And secondly, once you know what's not working for you, you can get rid of it, and devote that extra time and money to becoming more productive.

How do You Spend Your Time

If you are going to become more effective at time management you have to know what you are doing. If you have no idea about what you are doing, if you don't have a larger picture to work to, then you are going to be hopelessly lost. At all times you should have goals that you are working towards. You should have a clear purpose, you should know why you are doing, what you are doing.

First of all identify what your most important tasks are. These are the tasks that are critical to your success and which you should be spending the most time on. Your important tasks should take priority over everything else, for the simple reason that if you don't get them done, you will fail in what you are working on. If we use the 80 – 20 rule, you should be spending 80% of your time on 20% of your tasks. But is that what you are actually doing?

Despite knowing what we are supposed to be doing, it can be all too easy to subconsciously slip into bad habits. So in order find out how you currently spend your time, I want you to start recording everything that you on a daily basis. Just doing the exercise for a day might prove to be a real eye opener, but that's just one day. You can do it for longer if you want, but recording everything that you do in a week should give you an accurate picture as to how you spend your time.

By writing everything down, you have a record of your actions for the week. But what is important for you about this exercise, is that by taking the time to record everything, you have to think about what you have done on the day, and over the week. You might not have been consciously aware that you have not been making the best use of your time, but once you see it there in black and white, you will be forced to see it there in black and white, you will be forced to confront the fact that you have a time management problem.

It can be easy to ignore the fact that you have a problem. It's no good someone telling you that you have a problem, because you probably wouldn't believe them. But you cannot argue with the evidence.

Like any problem, you cannot begin to deal with it until you admit that you have a problem. You cannot identify the extent of your problems with time management until you record your personal actions. Once you can see that you have a problem, once you can identify your problems areas, then dealing with it should be relatively straightforward.

Create a To Do List

I got a bit curious and so I thought that would Google, "to do list." I really wasn't expecting to find much, but I was wrong. The vast amount of information available shows the importance of having a, to do list. Here's what Wikipedia says on the subject:

"Task list organization

Task lists are often tiered. The simplest tiered system includes a general to-do list (or task-holding file) to record all the tasks the person needs to accomplish, and a daily to-do list which is created each day by transferring tasks from the general to-do list.

Task lists are often prioritized:

- A daily list of things to do, numbered in the order of their importance, and done in that order one at a time until daily time allows, is attributed to consultant Ivy Lee(1877-1934) as the most profitable advice received by Charles M. Schwab(1862-1939), president of the Bethlehem Steel Corporation.

- An early advocate of "ABC" prioritization was Alan Lakein, in 1973. In his system "A" items were the most important ("A-1" the most important within that group), "B" next most important, "C" least important.

• A particular method of applying the ABC method assigns "A" to tasks to be done within a day, "B" a week, and 'C' a month.

• To prioritize a daily task list, one either records the tasks in the order of highest priority, or assigns them a number after they are listed ("1" for highest priority, "2" for second highest priority, etc.) which indicates in which order to execute the tasks. The latter method is generally faster, allowing the tasks to be recorded more quickly.

• Another way of prioritizing compulsory tasks (group A) is to put the most unpleasant one first. When it's done, the rest of the list feels easier. Groups B and C can benefit from the same idea, but instead of doing the first task (which is the most unpleasant) right away, it gives motivation to do other tasks from the list to avoid the first one.

• A completely different approach which argues against prioritising altogether was put forward by British author Mark Forster in his book "Do It Tomorrow and Other Secrets of Time Management". This is based on the idea of operating "closed" to-do lists, instead of the traditional "open" to-do list. He argues that the traditional never-ending to-do lists virtually guarantees that some of your work will be left undone. This approach advocates getting all your work done, every day, and if you are unable to achieve it helps you diagnose where you are going wrong and what needs to change.

Various writers have stressed potential difficulties with to-do lists such as the following:

• Management of the list can take over from implementing it. This could be caused by procrastination by prolonging the planning activity. This is akin to analysis paralysis. As with any activity, there's a point of diminishing returns.

• Some level of detail must be taken for granted for a task system to work. Rather than put "clean the kitchen", "clean the bedroom", and "clean the bathroom", it is more efficient to put "housekeeping" and save time spent writing and reduce the system's administrative load (each task entered into the system generates a cost in time and effort to manage it, aside from the execution of the task). The risk of consolidating tasks, however, is that "housekeeping" in this example may prove overwhelming or nebulously defined, which will either increase the risk of procrastination, or a mismanaged project.

• Listing routine tasks wastes time. If you are in the habit of brushing your teeth every day, then there is no reason to put it down on the task list. The same goes for getting out of bed, fixing meals, etc. If you need to track routine tasks, then a standard list or chart may be useful, to avoid the procedure of manually listing these items over and over.

• To remain flexible, a task system must allow for disaster. A company must be ready for a disaster. Even if it is a small disaster, if no one made time for this situation, it can metastasize, potentially causing damage to the company.

- To avoid getting stuck in a wasteful pattern, the task system should also include regular (monthly, semi-annual, and annual) planning and system-evaluation sessions, to weed out inefficiencies and ensure the user is headed in the direction he or she truly desires.

- If some time is not regularly spent on achieving long-range goals, the individual may get stuck in a perpetual holding pattern on short-term plans, like staying at a particular job much longer than originally planned."

As I hope that you can see, if you are not careful you can overcomplicate your to do list. You want to keep everything as simple as possible, because that will make it the most easily managed, and the easier things are for you, the more productive you will be.

You can buy templates, software and apps to create and to manage your to do list. Now I admit that they can be a valuable tool that gives you a fantastic ROI. But useful as they are in planning and controlling your greater picture, nothing beats the pure simplicity of just writing down your tasks for the day on a bit of paper. Try to keep things as simple as possible, because whenever you try to overcomplicate things then you will encounter problems.

For your long term goals, projects and strategies you will need a grander to do list, but for your day to day activities, a few lines on a bit of paper should be all that you need.

Whilst your, to do list looks at what tasks you need to do on a given day, your goal list is what you are looking to achieve overall. It can be a useful exercise to plan your goals for the year. Your yearly can be broken down into weekly and monthly goals. Please remember that these are goals and not tasks. Tasks are what you use to help you to accomplish your goals. By monitoring your goals you will be able to identify what progress you have made in achieving them, and any changes that you might need to make.

You can use your goal list in conjunction with your to do list, as it will help you to monitor your journey to your goals. Have weekly, monthly and yearly goals. Remember to keep your goals fluid, because you can't read the future and things can happen, things can change. So review your goals on a weekly and monthly basis.

Time Saving Tips

i. If you're in a meeting or somebody is talking about something, then listen to what is being said. Listening actively can be very difficult as your minds will automatically start to work on your response, or if you're not that interested in what's being said, your mind could just drift off. If your mind is not on what's being said then your body language will give you away, which will not endear you to the speaker. But more important, is that if you are not listening to what's being said, then you could miss information that is vital to your work. In order to keep your focus take notes, and don't be afraid to ask questions if you have something that needs clarifying.

ii. Get into the habit of writing out a, to do list, because with the best will in the world, (unless you are going to have a quiet day) you are never going to remember everything that you have to do. Keep the focus on your important tasks and try to make sure that you complete everything on your list. Review your list at the end of each day, celebrate your successes and if you had problems work out how you could have done things differently. Train yourself to go down your to do list without skipping or procrastinating your difficult tasks.

iii. When something works then examine it so that you know why. If you can see a way to improve it or to simplify the procedure, then do it, otherwise don't change a thing! Once you understand how it works, then you can look to see if you can apply it to other areas of your life and work.

If you have a process or a procedure that works then let it work. Anything that makes your life easier and improves productivity should be embraced with open arms.

iv. If you have something that needs doing then keep your focus on that task until you have finished it. You cannot concentrate on doing multiple tasks and expect to give them the attention that they need. If you concentrate on one task at a time you can finish it a lot quicker than you would otherwise, and then you can move on to the next and the next. When you have your attention scattered all over the place, you will be unable get you job done in a time efficient manner. Conversely, when your attention is laser focused you can expect to maintain constant forward momentum.

v. This should be a no brainer, but you would be surprised, or maybe not, at the people who don't seem to be able comprehend the concept. If you are doing something that is an unproductive waste of time, then don't do it!

vi. In any project there will be tasks that result in significant productivity and progress, and tasks that don't. If you are working on a project, or are working to a system, then look at what's producing results and what's not. There's no guarantee, but it's possible that you will uncover tasks that are unnecessary and that you can get rid of. You might not be able to eradicate all the time wasting minutiae, but if you can get rid of some then it will save you time.

vii. Before you embark on a project you plan it out and you prioritize. You prioritize your tasks for the day, week, month, and year. As you will no doubt be aware things can and do go wrong. When things go awry you need to stay confident in your ability to prioritize your tasks and just get on with it. If you lose confidence in yourself it can be easy to panic, and that's when mistakes happen. Just get on with your work and you will complete it far quicker than you would if you hit the panic button.

viii. As I have mentioned earlier, you have to concentrate on the important things first. The important things are what need finishing if you intend to complete your task. If you don't focus on the important thing then the job doesn't get done, and you don't achieve your goals.

ix. Think about what you are doing and work smarter and not harder! If you work a 60 hour week will you achieve more that someone who only works 40? The answer is probably not. The quantity of work that you put in is absolutely meaningless if it is not quality. If you plan what you are doing, know what you need to achieve, manage your distractions, and use a to do list, you will accomplish much more than someone who believes that if they only work for long enough, then they will get the job done. Don't waste your time putting in a crazy amount of work hours, work smarter, not harder!

x. It never ceasing to amaze me just how much power the prospect of reward has over us. No matter how small and insignificant the reward, people will work hard to win it because it's a visible symbol of their success. Following on from that, why not reward yourself for completing important or difficult tasks. Admittedly you have to exercise some self-discipline when doing this. If you know that the only way that you are going to give yourself a certain treat is when you've completed an important or difficult task, important or difficult things, then it's only human nature to push yourself hard to achieve it.

xi. It's vital that you don't lose sight of the bigger picture. You have long-terms goals that you want to achieve, and so long as you keep them in mind, everything that you do will take you closer to them. If you lose your focus, if you get distracted, if you ignore the important tasks in favor of the minutiae, and if you procrastinate, then you will put your goals on hold. Your goals could be career or productivity related, but when you lose sight of what you are aiming for then maybe you will miss a deadline, maybe you will lose a client, maybe you will lose out on your long-term goals completely.

xii. In order to remind you of what you're trying to achieve, put up signs stating your goals as a constant reminder of what you are trying to achieve. If you can't escape what you are trying to achieve then you'll not fall off the wagon. If you see reminders of your goals every day then that will make you more focused on achieving them, even if it's just so that you can get rid of those signs.

xiii. Evaluate your life goals once a month. Are you still on track or are you starting to drift. Is there anything that will give you the edge in achieving your goals? Or maybe things have changed, maybe you have a new job with fresh responsibilities, and you require fresh goals. Evaluating your life goals allows you to know where you are at that particular moment in time. If you don't know where you stand then you could find that you have taken a wrong turn, and that you might have wasted so much time, you might never achieve your goals.

Things change and you have to be prepared to change with them. We live in fast moving world and you cannot afford to waste time in losing your way.

xiv. Always be on the lookout new ideas and techniques that can help you save time. Maybe there is something technological, or maybe you come across a new system that you can implement, whatever it is, if it works then use it. Just remember that the simpler your time management system is, the easier it is to implement, and the more effective it is likely to be.

xv. If you have not done what you set out to do, will the world come to an end? I doubt it. The important thing is that you did your job to the best of your abilities. It's a fact of life that things happen, and sometimes that means that you are unable to complete your tasks to your satisfaction. The problem is that some people take it seriously and they will brood about it. Whilst they are having fun brooding and being miserable, they lose their focus. When they lose their focus on what they are doing their productivity suffers which makes them even more miserable.

If there are lessons to learn from what happened the learn them and move on. You're only human, so if you can't get something done, you can't get it done.

xvi. Whatever you don't dwell on your failures. What's happened has happened, there is nothing more you can do about it, so move on. If you made mistakes or have failed in the past then learn whatever lessons you can from those incidents and move on. By spending too much time brooding on the past you are not looking to what you can achieve in the future. If a lot of things have gone wrong for you, then you can reach the stage where you can be waiting for your next disaster instead of focusing on your work. You could become more cautious and take your time over everything that you do, and your productivity will suffer.

If you want to succeed you have to be decisive and you have to want to take action. Your past is your history and whilst it might be instructive to see what has gone before, it is irrelevant to your present situation. You cannot afford to spend your time being affected by the past, you have to be focused on your goals and what you will achieve in the future.

xvii. I've come across more than a few people who write that you should identify your weaknesses and work to strengthen them, and I can see why they do that. If you have weaknesses that are a problem for you then you need to deal with. However, given that none of us are perfect in every single thing that we do, is there any point to trying to deal with all of our weaknesses?

Personally I'm from the camp that says that you need to identify your strengths and strengthen them. Your strengths take priority over your weaknesses. You can strengthen your weak areas over time, but it's your strengths that will drive you forward to achieve your goals! Build on your successes. Try to steer clear of areas where you are at best mediocre, and concentrate on areas where your talents can create forward momentum.

If you can keep your main focus on the areas where you excel then you can only get better. You will have work colleagues who excel in the areas where you are weakest, so let them pursue those areas whilst you stick with your strengths. A team that can operate to its strengths is a strong team. If there isn't anyone who can take on your weaker tasks, then it could well be worth the expense to bring someone in.

I've a question for you. Would you rather waste time and energy trying to complete tasks for which you have no aptitude? Or would you rather bring someone in to deal with them, whilst you concentrated on where your talents lie?

xviii. If you want to succeed then you have to be positive, you have to be eternally optimistic. When you have a heavy workload it can be difficult trying to be positive but you have to try. If you can maintain a positive outlook, then no matter how difficult things get, you will always be able to confidently work towards the future. Your being positive an optimistic is work towards the future. Your being positive an optimistic is something that only you can do for yourself, no one else can do it for you!

If you are positive and optimistic then you are continually looking towards, and working towards the future. You have ambitious goals that you work towards, and you expect to achieve them. You try to make the most out of every moment because you want to succeed. Your productivity levels are high because you are motivated and you know that the only way to achieve your goals is to work hard, and to work smart. And no matter how bad things get you can always look forward to a brighter future.

The opposite of positive is negative, and negative individuals are a different breed to those who are positive. Their productivity levels are much lower because they are not interested. They have no goals, no drive, no energy, no ambition, and no motivation. Unlike those of a positive disposition who relish life, those who wallow in negativity take no joy from life. They exist rather than live. They don't care what happens, they just want to endure work and whilst there do no more than they have to. So be positive.

And Finally

If you are serious about achieving your goals then you have to practice good time management. If you don't practice good time management then you will struggle to get things done. If you are unable to meet deadlines through poor time management you could lose clients, and you will very likely fail to meet goals. We live in a fiercely competitive world where people demand rapid results. If you are unable work to the expectations of your role then you will struggle to fulfil it. Effective time management skills can give you the edge, but you have to take action in order to develop them.

Admittedly it can look complex, and it can be made far too overcomplicated, but Time Management isn't a particularly difficult discipline to follow.

The theory is simple. You need to create a workable system that is relevant to you and your situation, and put it into action. It's a simple as that. As I mentioned earlier you can automate things, but just be careful that you don't complicate what you do with too much software and too many systems. Keep it simple, keep it moving. If you Google time management software or time management systems, you will be swamped with information. The fact is that sometimes the simplest solutions are the best.

Once you have put into effect your time management system you should find yourself with free time, which will then leave you with a decision to make. Do you revel in the luxury of having less work to do, or do you find ways to further develop yourself and push your career forward. With effective time management you can increase your productivity, or you can use that extra time in training.

If you don't manage your time efficiently, then you end up spending a lot more than your contracted work hours in just trying to get your job done. That's not good for your productivity, your quality of life, and it's most certainly not good for your health. Don't forget that if your health becomes affected then so does your productivity.

By practicing good time management you more time for yourself and family. You cannot spend every hour you have at work, without it having a negative effect on you. You have to be able to relax and recharge your batteries. If you have more leisure time you will be more relaxed. If you are more rested, refreshed and relaxed, then your productivity will increase.

When you manage your time properly it means that you are not wasting any of it. When you are targeting where to spend your time you become more efficient. When you work more efficiently you get the job done quicker. If you can work through your tasks more quickly (and don't forget accurately) then your productivity will rise.

If you are struggling to complete your tasks then it's very difficult to remain positive, and there is every chance that you will start to brood on your inability to do your job. If you slip into a negative mindset then your self-esteem will drop and you will struggle even more to complete your tasks.

Don't whatever you do forget to takes breaks, and to have a lunch break. No matter how good you are, you cannot spend the whole day working and expect to retain your concentration, your motivation and productivity. Throughout the day you need to spend time away from your desk to clear your head, stretch your legs and relax. It might mean time away from your tasks, but when your return fresh and alert, it is more than worth it.

The most important break of your working day is lunch, and far too many people work through it. I'm not sure why, but I used to have a problem with taking lunch breaks. The mornings were fine, but as the day wore on my mind would slow down and I would become less efficient, that obviously had an effect on my productivity levels.

Just as a car needs fuel to make it work, so your body needs food. You should have had breakfast which will have given you the energy that you need to last until your lunch. Your lunch will provide you with the energy that your body to last until your evening meal. If you deny yourself your lunch break then you are denying yourself then energy that you need for your body and your mind to operate efficiently. Not having a lunch break is a false economy! When you come back from lunch you are rested, refreshed and ready to take on the world. If you miss lunch then your performance will not be as effective as it could be, and it will decrease as the day wears on.

I once heard of a company in I think it was Manchester in the U.K. They didn't just require their staff to have lunch, they ordered them out of the office until their lunch break was over. That must have been fun for everyone in winter, but they would only do that if there were some benefits to be gained for themselves, and their staff.

Once you have put into practice your new time management skills and started reaping the benefits from them then you will feel both positive and optimistic. If you start to enjoy regular success at work, your self-esteem will rise. You will become more confident and positive because you will know that you can and will succeed. And needless to say, your productivity will rise.

You go to work because you need to make money. You have bills to pay and things to buy. The more successful you are at work the more money you will make. Everyone has their own personal and professional goals. It's all really quite simple. The better that you are able to manage your work life, the closer you will get to achieving your goals.

You Can Beat Procrastination

You just don't know it... YET

By

Michael Finlayson

What is Procrastination?

Given that this is a book on how to beat procrastination, I thought that it would be a good idea to see how it is viewed through the eyes of others. The following chapter is made up of various quotes on the nature of time and procrastination, as well as a fascinating article from Wikipedia.

"Procrastination is the bad habit of putting off until the day after tomorrow what should have been done the day before yesterday."

Napoleon Hill

It's great to say that I'll do it tomorrow and then tomorrow never comes. But if you don't do it now, then when will you do it?

This is the Wikipedia description.

"In Psychology, procrastination refers to the act of replacing more urgent actions with tasks less urgent, or doing something from which one derives enjoyment, and thus putting off impending tasks to a later time. In accordance with Freud, the pleasure principle may be responsible for procrastination; humans prefer avoiding negative emotions, and delaying a stressful task. The concept that humans work best under pressure provides additional enjoyment and motivation to postponing a task. Some psychologists site such behavior as a mechanism for coping with the anxiety associated with starting or completing any task or decision.

Other psychologists indicate that anxiety is just as likely to get people to start working early as late and the focus should be impulsiveness. That is, anxiety will cause people to delay only if they are impulsive.

Schraw, Wadkins, and Olafson have proposed three criteria for a behavior to be classified as procrastination: it must be counterproductive, needless, and delaying. Similarly, Steel (2007) reviews all previous attempts to define procrastination, indicating it is "to voluntarily delay an intended course of action despite expecting to be worse off for the delay.

Procrastination may result in stress, a sense of guilt and crisis, severe loss of personal productivity, as well as social disapproval for not meeting responsibilities or commitments. These feelings combined may promote further procrastination. While it is regarded as normal for people to procrastinate to some degree, it becomes a problem when it impedes normal functioning. Chronic procrastination may be a sign of an underlying psychological disorder. Such procrastinators may have difficulty seeking support due to social stigma and the belief that task-aversion is caused by laziness, low willpower or low ambition. On the other hand many regard procrastination as a useful way of identifying what is important to us personally way of identifying what is important to us personally as it is rare to procrastinate when one truly values the task at hand.

Psychological

Psychologists continue to debate the causes of procrastination. Drawing on clinical work, there appears to be a connection with issues of anxiety, low sense of self-worth, and a mentality. On the other hand, drawing on meta-analytical correlational work, anxiety and perfectionism have no – or at best an extremely weak – connection with procrastination. Instead, procrastination is strongly connected with lack of self-confidence (e.g., low self-efficacy, or learned helplessness) or disliking the task (e.g., boredom and apathy). The strongest connection to procrastination, however, is impulsiveness.

These characteristics are often used as measures of the personality trait conscientiousness whereas anxiety and irrational beliefs (such as perfectionism) are aspects of the personality trait neuroticism. Accordingly, Lee, Kelly and Edwards (2006) indicated that neuroticism has no direct links to procrastination and that any relationship is fully mediated by conscientiousness.

Based on integrating several core theories of motivation as well as meta-analytic research on procrastination is the temporal motivational theory. It summarizes key predictors of procrastination (i.e., expectancy, value and impulsiveness) into a mathematical equation.

Physiological

Research on the physiological roots of

procrastination mostly surrounds the role of the prefrontal cortex. Consistent with the notion that procrastination is strongly related to impulsiveness, this area of the brain is responsible for executive brain functions such as planning, impulse control, and attention, and acts as a filter by decreasing distracting stimuli from other brain regions. Damage or low activation in this area can reduce an individual's ability to filter out distracting stimuli, ultimately resulting in poorer organization, a loss of attention and increased procrastination. This is similar to the prefrontal lobe's role inattention-deficit hyperactivity disorder, where underactivation is common.

Mental health

For some people, procrastination can be persistent and tremendously disruptive to everyday life. For these individuals, procrastination may be symptomatic of a psychological disorder such as depression or neurological disorder such as ADHD. Therefore, it is important for people whose procrastination has become chronic and is perceived be debilitating, to seek out a trained therapist or psychiatrist to see if an underlying mental health issue may be present.

Perfectionism

Traditionally, procrastination has been associated with perfectionism, a tendency to negatively evaluate outcomes and one's own performance, intense fear and avoidance of evaluation of one's abilities by others, heightened social self-consciousness and anxiety, recurrent low mood, and "workaholism". According to Robert B. Slaney adaptive perfectionists (when perfectionism is egosyntonic) were less likely to procrastinate than non-perfectionists, while maladaptive perfectionists (people who saw their perfectionism as a problem; i.e., when perfectionism is egodystonic) had high levels of procrastination (and also of anxiety). Accordingly, meta-analytic review of 71 studies by Steel (2007) indicate that typically perfectionists actually procrastinate slightly less than others, with "the exception being perfectionists who were also seeking clinical counseling."

I think it fair to say that you won't get a better description of procrastination than that provided by Wikipedia. Procrastination can be something that we laugh about, or that some will sneer about, but after reading this excerpt from Wikipedia I hope that you appreciate that procrastination can be serious. Admittedly it doesn't affect us all at the extreme levels, but it does show you what can happen if you can't beat procrastination. Don't waste your life. If you do have a problem with procrastination, then you need to come up with a strategy that will help you to beat it.

"Procrastination is the thief of time."

Charles Dickens

Agreed! Time is our most precious commodity, once it's gone it's gone, and none of us can afford to waste our time by procrastinating. If you are procrastinating, then you are not doing what you need to do in order to move forward. When you stop moving forward the world will still carry on around you, you will still get older, but you will be held in stasis.

"You may delay, but time will not."

Benjamin Franklin

Time really doesn't care if you are able to keep up with it or not. Time is a great leveller because no matter who you are, rich or poor it will not wait for you. You waste your own time at your peril

"Time is an equal opportunity employer. Each human being has exactly the same number of hours and minutes every day. Rich people can't buy more hours. Scientists can't invent new minutes. And you can't save time to spend it on another day. Even so, time is amazingly fair and forgiving. No matter how much time you've wasted in the past, you still have an entire tomorrow."

Dennis Waitley

This is very true. Each new day we have a fresh opportunity to go out and really do something, and that holds true for whoever you are. Just don't forget that the more fresh days that you waste, the more you program your mind to inaction.

The mind is a truly wonderful thing, just so along as you keep it disciplined. If you lose control of that discipline then you put your ambition and goals at risk.

"Nothing is so fatiguing as the eternal hanging on of an uncompleted task."

William James

Good point. When you've something that needs doing, that you know you will have to do at some point but don't, it is tiring because you can't move forward until it's dealt with.

"I'm a big believer in putting things off, In fact, I even put off procrastinating."

Ella Varner

I love this quote, although it is one that can be adapted. I remember being in a webinar once listening to someone talk about procrastination, and he talked about procrastinating your procrastination.

If you are struggling with procrastination, then sometimes taking a light hearted look at the problem can help you more than a serious in-depth analysis. So if you have problems try putting them off, or procrastinating them. Save them up until you've nothing better to do.

"Lack of confidence, sometimes alternating with unrealistic dreams of heroic success, often leads to procrastination, and many studies suggest that procrastinators are self-handicappers: rather than risk failure, they prefer to create conditions that make success impossible, a reflex that of course creates a vicious cycle."

James Surowiecki

You need to believe in yourself. You need to be a realist, there are some things that you will never be able to do, although that shouldn't stop you reaching for the stars, just so long as you take action!

"If not now, when?"

Tina Williams

If you have something to do, then do it. If you don't do it then your task will still be waiting for you. It might be a task that you loathe, but the longer that you take to start your task, the more difficult it will be to complete it. So when are you going to do it?

If you want to achieve success you have to plan for it. If you want success you will have to step outside of your comfort zone. Success doesn't give a damn about whether you want to do something or not, it demands that you give your all. If you genuinely want to be successful then you have to create the conditions where that can happen, and then, for without this you will achieve nothing, you have to take action. And yes I realize that taking action can be difficult, it can be far easier to just sit back and watch the world, and all your hopes and dreams just drift on by.

Unless you are born with a silver spoon in your mouth then you are going to have to work hard to achieve success, you are going to have to commit your all. If you want to achieve success there is no room for excuses, there is only room for you to take positive action and for you to create forward momentum in your life.

Procrastination

I don't know about you, but at any one time I usually have plenty of projects to keep me occupied. Once in a while that list can grow far too quickly because I can find it very difficult to stick at the task, consequently and for whatever bizarre, irritating reason, and despite the fact that I know what I have to do, I find other pointless tasks to pursue. Despite being more than aware that doing really useful things such as playing games on Facebook is getting me nowhere, I still do it, and I can still find some incredibly weak reason to justify what I am doing.

How about yourself? Are you late for appointments, do you struggle to meet deadlines, are things that you have to do but you just can't stomach them, so you forget about them? Do you keep putting things off even though you know that you have to do them or that you need to do them? I always find it strange that even though something is clearly in our best interests, we can still find reasons to prevaricate. Are you ever late for appointments, do you accidently forget about things that you have to do? And I guess that the worst one has to be having something that you really want to do, something that you're really motivated to do, and yet you are struggling to get started, and the more that you want to do it the more difficult it becomes to knuckle down and take action.

Does it annoy you as it does me, this frustrating inability to get started on a project, this inability to get stuck in to whatever task or project that you're working on. The worst thing about it is that you want to do it, but it's a Battle Royale to make any forward progress. It can be frustrating knowing that you have the ability and talent to achieve your goals, it can be even more frustrating when you see people pushing ahead and cruising past you.

I think that perhaps the worst thing about procrastination is that you are only putting off the inevitable, and you are quite aware that you are only putting off the inevitable! At some point you are going to have to knuckle down and do whatever it is that you've been avoiding like the plague. I was listening to a webinar at some point in the past, and the guy who was the main speaker had a fantastic solution for procrastination. So, instead of procrastinating all those necessary tasks that you are going to have to do anyway, why not procrastinate your procrastination. Think about it, if you're going to procrastinate it anyway, why not save it up for a time of your choosing, such as when you're watching the T.V. I'm having fun trying to get my mind hooked into this concept, but I'm getting there.

There are probably a variety of reasons as to why you procrastinate. You might have very good reasons for putting something off for another day, something might have happened to knock your schedule out of sync, character building things like this are all part the rich tapestry of life. On the other hand, your reasons may be less than ideal. You might have poor time management skills. You could lack confidence in your ability to complete a task. You might struggle to set goals and keep to what you have planned. You might be a perfectionist and so will only deal with what you can do well. You might have programmed yourself to believe that you don't have any willpower. You might have low self-esteem. Whatever the reason for your procrastination, it can be dealt with and you can beat procrastination.

By the time that you have finished this book you will have a greater understanding of the main causes of procrastination, and you will know how to deal with them. Knowing what's been holding you back for so long is a massive game changer. Once you have identified what's been holding you back you can deal with it and then you can take control of your life and start building up some forward momentum.

Okay my friend, irrespective of what you want to achieve there is a way for you to do it. At this point I should say that I'm talking about realistic goals here, and not say being able to buy the White House for $1. This book is all about you and what you can achieve. By the time you finish this book I want you to be able to understand what's been holding you back, and once you've figured that out I want you to be able to come up with an actionable plan that can help you to achieve your goals.

The Joys of Procrastination

It all begins with attitude. It could be your attitude to goal setting, it could be how you handle time management, but whatever your situation it all starts out with your attitude. Which when you think about it makes good sense, because your attitude to a task or a project decides how you will approach it and deal with it. If you move forward with a positive attitude then you will achieve your goals and move on. However, if you approach a situation with a more negative attitude, then you will struggle to achieve your goals. I'm not saying that you approach tasks with a deliberately negative attitude, it's more likely to be that you've subconsciously picked up some negativity towards that specific situation. It's important that you realize that we all have our own personal strengths and weaknesses, and the odds are that it's some of your weaknesses that are the root cause of your procrastination.

In order to get the ball rolling, take action and actually do something! Make it something which requires drive and energy from you in order to see it through, something that requires you to exercise some willpower in order to stay on track! It doesn't matter what it is, but get out from the safety of your comfort zone. It doesn't matter if you do this at or away from work, you have to want to take the first step. Once you have taken that first step then it becomes a bit easier to take the next and the next and the next.

You know something. I'm one of those who have

been trying to create an online future. I got myself started on the affiliate route and it was a long time before I admitted to myself that I was going to need a website. Once I admitted that I needed a site it took me an age before I finally took action and got my first one up. Personally I only ever use Wordpress blogs and there is nothing easier to set up. I knew that I had to do it, but it looked far too technical to me, and I am not the most technically adept of people. I kept on finding excuses not to do it, to put it politely they were pretty pathetic excuses, but I listened to them. I could always find some pointless tasks to do, these tasks would give me the illusion that I was working hard, but they didn't bring me one step closer to achieving my goals. There have been a few occasions when I really needed to push the content of some of my sites, but I didn't because I wanted to wait, and wait, and wait until I had everything perfect.

No matter whom you are, if you don't have the confidence in your abilities then it's far too easy to talk yourself into inaction. If you have something that needs doing don't think about it, just do it. If you never try something then you will never know what you could have achieved. If you do not take action and do what needs doing then how can you move forward? By not taking action you will be held in stasis, and there you will stay until you deal with your procrastination. Your uncompleted tasks will stop you from moving forward to complete your goals.

If you procrastinate on a regular basis then you will program your mind to accept defeat, and once your mind becomes comfortable with your acceptance of defeat, then it will be difficult to break that habit, although not impossible.

One thing that I've noticed about any technical challenges that I've had, is that once I stopped wasting my time finding reasons why I shouldn't try, the challenge always turned out to be much more simple than I had led myself to believe. No matter how simple the challenge was, I felt good about having dealt with it. And having managed to achieve something me self-esteem got a boost, as did my self-confidence. Whether you like it or not, you are much more capable than you let yourself believe, you just need to find a way of unlocking your potential.

Don't think about it just to it. Remember, if not now ther **WHEN!** The more that you think about a task or a project, the more you will dither and procrastinate. The longer you wait to take action, the longer your mind has to tell you that you're just not up to the job. You have to take responsibility for your task and just do it. Or of course you could always dither and vacillate for an age or so, wasting your precious time in the process. And before you say anything, yes I do know that it can be easier said than done.

You've probably all heard of the saying, step out of your comfort zone. This is what you are going to have to do if you want to beat procrastination. When your mind has become used to your acceptance of defeat, when it has become overly used to just ticking along, it doesn't like to be stretched, it doesn't like to be pushed, and it will whisper words of defeat to you in order to stop all this aggravation. If you want to succeed you have to step outside the comfort zone, you have to push yourself and to make demands of your mind. It's not easy, but you can do it.

Do you actually know, deep down in your heart of hearts just what you want for yourself? Are people all around you moving forward in their lives with a purpose, but you're still struggling to know what you want? It can be difficult in life to know what you need to be happy and to find contentment in your life. It's all too easy to end up following the crowd, it's comfortable to be a part of the crowd, it's great to share similar tastes, ideas and whatever, but is it really you? If you don't know what you really want, then you are going to struggle to devote the time and energy to what needs doing.

Without goals you will drift and you will have no real sense of purpose, and that would be such a waste.

Who are you? Do you actually know? Are you one of those people who live for the moment? Do you enjoy a happy carefree existence, are you a firm believer in making no plans for the future, and are you content to let tomorrow take care of itself? A wonderfully Utopian way to live assuming that is that you can sustain it. The thing about the carefree lifestyle is that it is averse to setting goals, and without being able to set goals and work towards those goals, then how can you expect to move forward in life and achieve the lifestyle that you want?

I'm guessing that at some point most if not all of us have been guilty of this, and that's setting such demanding goals that we scare ourselves off from achieving them. Having ambition is great, and it's what helps to move you forward, but you need to be a realist as well. By all means set yourself goals that will see you reaching for the stars, but be wise enough to realize that you stand the best chance of achieving your goals if you work towards them one step at a time.

Think about it. You have your big scary goals that will take time and energy to achieve. If you look at the goal in its entirety then it could be a scary thing, you could convince yourself that you'll never achieve it, so why bother trying. On the other hand if you break down your goals into achievable steps then you are no longer looking at a long, hard slog. Instead you are looking at something that you can achieve on step at a time.

Any goal can be broken down into smaller, more easily achievable steps. It's psychologically easier to take one step at a time than it is just trying to throw yourself at a goal. It doesn't matter how big the steps are. With each step your confidence will grow. With each step, your belief in yourself and your ability to achieve will grow. With each step your motivation and your willpower will grow. It's amazing what you can achieve by taking one forward step.

You should always do your best to achieve the best possible result, but that doesn't mean that you should get overly concerned with perfection. Perfection isn't all that it's made up to be. If you are

93

unfortunate enough to become a perfectionist then you can take things way to personally, and you can lack the confidence to try new things. Probably the saddest thing about perfectionism is that if you don't do everything perfectly then you're a failure.

Have you heard that to err is to be human? We all make mistakes, we all have things that go wrong for us, but the important thing is that if something goes wrong then you learn from it, and then you move on. I've had more than my share of learning experiences but I keep moving forward. If you are afraid of failure then you are afraid of life and that will hold you back, it will make you afraid to try, and that will waste your life. The important thing is that you try and that you keep on trying no matter what. For those of you who are worried about failure, the only failure that you should be concerned about is in never having tried.

I guess that if you are not confident in yourself then you can end up comparing yourself with others, and that can bring you grinding to a halt. It's all too easy to look at others and brood on how much more successful in life they are, how much better educated they are, how much more attractive they are, and how much more socially adept a person they are. Negative thinking like that can destroy your confidence and self-belief. Those thoughts can break you down bit by bit until you reach the point of thing why should I bother, where's the point? The reality of life is that we all have our own talents and abilities that are unique to us, and in order to move forward in life, we need to work to our own strengths and weaknesses. Who cares about how successful other people are, don't waste your time comparing yourself with others, the only one that should concern you is you! And by focusing on you, you will be able to look at how you can become rather successful, rather than wasting your time and being jealous about the success of others.

There will be those of you to whom this next statement will come as a great shock. You might find it hard to believe, but you can't do it all yourself! I am truly awful when it comes to asking for help, even though it means that by doing so I will be able to move forward more quickly. I'm stubborn, I have to try to do things myself, and as a consequence I can waste a lot of time, and that's time that could be better spent in pursuing my goals.

You may be stubborn (I most certainly am), you might hate asking for help, but when help, support and advice is there just waiting for the asking, then you're a fool to yourself if you don't take it up. And I know, "Mike, practice what you preach!!!" We all have better things to do with our time than wasting it. Co-operation and support from your work colleagues, your friends and family is no big deal, it's natural to give and to receive support, all you have to do is ask.

It's natural to give and to receive support, all you have to do, and this can be the tricky bit, is to ask for it.

Do you ever wish that there were 96 hours in the day instead of a paltry 24 (I do)? How good are you with time management? Are you able to prioritize what needs doing or are you a bit happy go lucky? Not being able to prioritize can cause you to struggle, especially if you hone in on those wonderful, less important tasks that allow you to think that you're actually doing something (which in one respect that is true, as wasting your time is indeed doing something), rather than you concentrating on what's important and actually achieving something.

No one can predict the future except, unless you are lucky, one thing. Have you noticed how life has this irritating habit of making your carefully laid plans go astray? That's something that I noticed a long time ago. In so far as is possible you have to plan everything out. If you cannot plan, and if you are unable to adjust your plan when life decides to have some fun with you, then you can and will have problems. Still, at least time management and prioritization are teachable subjects. That is, just so long as you can allow yourself some flexibility in your thinking!

If you lack the skillset needed to do something it can dent your confidence, and lead you to waste time doing pointless time consuming tasks, or it might cause you not to try at all. I am not the techiest of people, and when I'm faced with some task that appears beyond me, instead of getting help I tend to ignore that task for as long as possible. I know that at some point I am going to have to deal with it, but just not yet. And as I've already mentioned, situations like this are a source of constant irritation and frustration for me, especially when I discover just how easy that particular task was.

You have to remember that just because you **THINK** that you can't do something, it doesn't necessarily mean that you're right! There is every chance that your lack of confidence in your abilities has colored your perceptions, so you tell yourself that it's far too difficult, instead of looking at the problem and working out how to deal with it. You need to believe in yourself and your abilities. Whether you like it or not, there is more to you than you let yourself believe.

If you have a problem or have come up against a barrier to your forward progress, then by taking positive action to deal with it, you still have forward momentum. If there is something that is outside your skillset then ask for help, the world won't come to an end if you do. You might not like asking for help, but by doing so you will deal more quickly with whatever is impeding your progress, and then you can continue the pursuit of your goals. You never know, you might even learn something.

You have to identify and recognize your strengths and weaknesses. You need to recognize your weaknesses to see in which areas you can improve and maybe get some more training.

You have to realize that you can't know everything and do everything. Instead of trying to do everything, focus in on your strengths, develop them, and use them to your best possible advantage. When you concentrate on what you're good at you will strengthen your belief in your abilities. When you are confident in your abilities it gives the boost that you need to pursue your goals, and the confidence to achieve them.

I don't know if you have allowed yourself believe that you possess not one jot of willpower, if that's the case then you are a member of one of the largest clubs in the world. If it's the case that you struggle to engage your latent will power, then no big deal, the world is not going to end just because you have yet to wake up your willpower. Willpower is one of those things that you can develop by a combination of self-discipline and facing up to the fears that are holding you back.

Just because you think that you don't have any willpower, it's doesn't necessarily mean that you are right. Take a look at the things that you have done over your life. Look for the evidence that you have used willpower. Look at the circumstances and see if there is anything that can be applied to your current situation. At the very least realize that if your will was strong once, it can be so again. It's just dormant, and waiting for you to wake it up again.

Here's something for you to think about. Who are you? Once you can identify your strengths and weaknesses, once you are able to identify your skills and talents, once you are able to identify your own behavioral pattern, then with this knowledge and understanding about your good self, you'll be able to develop the skills that you need in order to help you to stop procrastinating, and to get on with your life.

Time Management

It's a fact that as a general rule, we don't appreciate our health until we lose it and I can say that from experience. Once your health is gone, it's gone. Time is probably our most precious possession, one that we never appreciate because it's there. We all get 24 hours in the day to use as best we can, and once we've used up that 24 hours we will never see it again. We live busy lives and time can seem to rush by at a ferocious rate. It's bad enough if we don't make the best use of our time away from work, but when it happens at work then we can struggle. If you're struggling to make the best use of your time at work then you could be struggling with your job, which naturally enough means that your stress levels will start to rise, which will further exacerbate your problems.

Whilst I'm not going to do an in-depth analysis of time management I can give you some easy to follow steps that will help your through your day.

Have Breakfast and Lunch

Just as a car needs fuel to make it work, the human body needs food, and it needs to be topped up with food. For reasons that I cannot begin to understand there are far too many people who start the day without breakfast. Maybe they'll have some nice unhealthy snacks to keep them going until lunch, or maybe they won't have anything but a cup of coffee because they don't want to put any weight, aye right. When you sleep your body's metabolism slows down, and it won't speed up again until you eat food. Breakfast has been called the most important meal of the day for good reason! The food you eat will give you the energy that you need for your body to remain fully charged until lunch. If you don't eat breakfast where will you get the energy that you need to remain sharp and active? How do you expect your mind to function at its best if you don't give your body the fuel that it needs?

And then we come to lunch. How many of you skip lunch because you're just too busy? I used to have that problem until I learned better. By skipping lunch you miss out on feeding your body the energy that it needs, and no, chocolate bars are not the kind of energy that your body or your mind needs. When you take a lunch break it's important that you take it away from your desk. I remember hearing of one company, I forget their name, who ordered their people out of the office at lunch time. By taking a break from your desk you get the opportunity to relax, to chill out, and to think about anything but what you are working on. Once you've had your break you will go back to your desk feeling refreshed, invigorated and focused.

You might think that you save time by skipping breakfast, and you might think that it's a more productive use of your time to work through lunch, I hope that I've shown you that it's **NOT!**

You Need a Plan

You don't just need to keep your body working, you need a plan. By a plan I mean the short, medium and long-term goals that will carry your forward. If you want to make the best use of your time you need to know what you want out of life both in personal and career terms. Do you know what you want to be, or are you wandering along in a happy go lucky style? Have you established what your priorities in life are, or have you never considered what is important to you?

It's important to establish your main long-term goals first because you need something to work to, something to fire your ambition and determination, something that will keep you motivated It's important to establish your main long-term goals first because you need something to work to, something to fire your ambition and determination, something that will keep you motivated through the good times and the bad.

Once you know what you're aiming for then you need to know how to get there, so work it out, create a plan out all the steps that you need to take in order to achieve your main goals, and make those your short and medium-term goals. Once you know what you are working too then you will find it much easier to plan things out, and you will be much more focused on what you need to do in order to achieve your goals.

Apart from you needing a plan in your personal life, you can also apply it to a work situation. For example if you have a project which is your long-term goal. You then break down what's needed to completed it into simple steps (or as simple as is possible) which then become your short and medium-term goals.

The one thing about plans, whether they relate to your own life or work is that life has this irritating habit of throwing a spanner in the works. Unless you have some kind of special powers you cannot see into the future, you don't know if everything will go smoothly, and you don't know if things will change. Your plan needs to be flexible, if needs to cover all the potential eventualities that you can think off and plan for. If your plan is flexible then if thing do go wrong then you will be ready with a new course of action, and you won't be running around wondering what to do. Even if something unexpected happens, the fact that you are approaching everything with a flexible mind set will help you to deal with the situation and make any necessary changes. Remember to keep your plan updated so that you know where you are at any given point of time.

Make a List

I'm assuming that just like me you're a mere mortal, unless off course you have some kind of psychic powers? Being mortal you will hopefully realize that you don't know everything and you can't remember everything. I remember this first time that I was told to MAKE A LIST. I was out for the day with one of my managers, and up to that point I never even thought of making a list, I would have a rough idea of what I needed to do, if I did it I did it, if I didn't I didn't. When I was told to start making a daily to do list, it was as if the clouds had cleared and the sun was beaming down on me.

Think about it, unless you are having a quiet day then there is no way that you will remember everything. Without a list the odds on you tackling your tasks in order of priority are slim. Without a list you will not be working to a plan you will be working more to impulse, and doing things because it feels right at the time is hardly the most efficient use of your time.

You have your short, medium and long-term goals. Once you have those goals you break them up into the steps that you have to follow to achieve them. Think of them as mini goals. But mini goals or not, you still have to be organized if you want to complete them.

If you are serious about achieving your goals then you need to be organized in your pursuit of them. Having a to do list helps you to give some structure to your steps, it allows you to deal with everything in order of priority (don't forget your lunch), it helps you to work out schedules and timings, it keeps you organized.

Regardless of what you're trying to achieve, if you know what you need to do that day, that week, that month, it makes it a lot easier to get the job done. With a, to do list, you can do that.

You don't have to turn everything off. You can respond to every email, every Skype notification, every personal phone call and text. You can waste hours playing games and keeping in touch with your friends on Facebook. But tell me this, given that time is such a precious resource, where are you going to find the time to replace that which you lost playing about on unnecessary communication platforms?

Work Smarter

Let's say that you are contracted to work 40 hours a week. For the sake of argument, your commitment and dedication, let's say that you work an extra 15 hours a week, my personal record is a 96 hour week, and strangely enough I had a car crash after which my perspective changed. My question is this. By diligently working those 15 extra hours a week, will you get the job done quicker and (okay so I thought of another) and will you do a better job?

Just because you are working more doesn't mean that you will do a better job. You could come to grudge all those extra hours struggling away for a company that you could come to loathe. By spending all the extra time working you might not give yourself enough time to relax and recharge outside of work. If you're coming to work tired and drained then you will not be operating at your best. If you are struggling at work then your stress levels could start to rise, and if the further decreases your performance then you might not have a job. It's a bit of a nightmare scenario, but as I'm sure you'll agree, it could happen.

Think quality over quantity. If you want to achieve you goals will you need to give your very best, or could it be that a stressed, pressurized approach get you're the results that you need?

If you want to achieve your goals you are going to

have to learn to prioritize your tasks. You have to be able to deal with the important tasks first, they take priority over everything else because these are the tasks that will ensure that you achieve your goals. You cannot afford to pick and choose what you want to do, apart from being a woefully inefficient way to spend your time, it will likely mean that you struggle to complete your projects and achieve your goals.

Categorize your tasks along the lines of urgent, important, average, minutiae.

Urgent: These are tasks that are urgent could occur when something unexpected happens, or maybe you have ignored and important goal for too long and it has become urgent. All being well you shouldn't have to deal with too many of these, but it's always good to be prepared for the possibility. Always make sure that you have a contingency plan prepared. Don't keep your plan static, make sure that it is fluid and keep it constantly updated.

Important: These are the tasks that if you don't achieve them then you will not achieve your goals. These tasks take priority and they should always be your main focus. Even if you have to delegate some of these tasks, you still need to keep an eye on them.

Average: These are tasks that although not critical to your success, nevertheless are still important for your success. These tasks need completing but they don't have the same level of urgency as your important goals. These tasks can be delegated.

Minutiae: These tasks are all the bits and pieces that need doing, but the world won't end if you don't do them right now. These tasks can be delegated.

There will be tasks that you loathe and despise. It might be that they're a wonderful cure for insomnia, or it could be that you genuinely hate doing them. If at all possible delegate them, but if you can't delegate them then you are going to have to get stuck into them. This is the point where you willpower and motivation kicks in. If you are serious about achieving your goals then you will grit your teeth and get working. If you are really struggling with them the look at why you hate them so much, is there any real reason for your loathing? If these are important tasks then there is a lot riding on them, so try to find ways to refocus your mind on how you approach them, try to find the positives in your loathsome tasks, at the very least completing them will bring your one step closer to achieving your goals.

Time is too precious a thing to waste by procrastinating it. What I have given you are some very simple tricks to help you make the most of your time. Yes I know that they are very much based on common sense, that irritating thing that we all too often ignore, but if you take action on them they can often ignore, but if you take action on them they can help you. Some of these points will be repeated later on because there are some things that are worth repeating.

What Are Your Strengths & Weaknesses?

Let me ask you a question. Who are you? Do you know who you are? Have you achieved what you have hoped for, or are you still trying to find your way? Do you know how the world perceives you? Could it be that the world has a better opinion of you than you do yourself? Probably.

I think it's true to say about the vast majority of us that we don't know who are, and we don't know what we are capable of. You don't get that kind of knowledge until you have been tested to your limits. As a consequence of this we tend not to be aware of our full potential, and as a consequence of that we all too often hold ourselves back and not perform to the levels that we are capable of. I hope that by the end of this chapter that you will realize that there is more to you than you have let yourself believe.

In the coming chapter I will be asking you questions about things that you might not have considered before, but answer them as best you can, because they will give you an insight into what you are comfortable with.

If you identify things that you're comfortable with, if you find things that you enjoy doing, then you will find it much easier to overcome procrastination, after all, who has problems doing things that they enjoy? Not me that's for certain.

What Can You Do?

The point of this exercise is to get you focusing on what you can do, and not just on what you think that you can do. The easiest way is to do this is to look at a project that you have worked on in the past. It really doesn't matter what the project was, it could be something at work, in the home or even in a social situation. The important thing is to look at a successful project. Once you can evaluate your contribution to the project, you will have a much clearer of what you can do, and you should be able to identify any possible weak areas that require building up.

In order to help you through the process I've come up with a series of questions. Please remember to be brutally honest with your answers. To kick the process off, start by working through these questions:

i. How did you manage to achieve a successful result? If this was a group effort, what was your contribution?

ii. What skills did you have to use to achieve the result?

ii. What skills did you have to use to achieve the result?

iii. Did you have any support or was this a solo project?

iv. Unless you're lucky, there are usually some kinds of problems that you have to deal with. How were you able to deal with yours?

v. There must have been specific things that significantly contributed to the success of your project. What were they, was there equipment that was particularly useful, were there members of the team who were exceptional, or did you have to bring a specialist in?

vi. Think about all the different stages of the project and try to remember what you were feeling at the time. Did you experience frustration, elation, or did you just get on with it?

vii. How did your strengths and weaknesses come in to play during the project, and try to match them to the various points of the project? This can be a difficult thing to do, but see how many different ones you can come up with.

viii. If you had to do the same thing again, what would you do, would you change anything or keep it as it was? What skills would you bring across to the new project and is there any particular task that you would avoid like the plague?

ix. Okay, so you completed a successful project, what did you learn from it?

x. This last step is especially useful if it was a work based project. As your work colleagues, or anyone who was a part of the project the same questions.

Compare their answers with yours, and see if there is anything to be learned from them.

How Are You at Goal Setting?

In this exercise all you need to do is to identify the statement that most closely matches your attitude to goal setting.

i. I'm a great believer in planning everything as much as is possible.

ii. Who cares about tomorrow, I live for today and tomorrow can take care of itself.

iii. I believe in planning ahead as far as is possible so that I know what each holds for me.

iv. Don't you just love surprises!

v. I have a vision for work and at home which keeps my life moving forward.

vi. Change... yeeeurch, only if I have a plan to help me to deal with it.

Admittedly, that might have been a slightly irreverent look at the different styles of planning, but that's me. You see, it really doesn't matter if you need to plan everything doesn't matter if you need to plan everything out, or if you're a spontaneous kind of person, there is a planning style that is perfectly suited to whoever you are.

Regardless of kind of planner you are, the thing that separates the planner from the plodder is that you have the flexibility to adjust your plan and your life whenever life throws a spanner in the works.

What about Your willpower and Motivation Levels?

I suppose that will power and motivation could be two separate sections, but then when you look at them, the more will power that you have the less likely that you are to give up, the less likely you are to get distracted and fall of the motivational wagon. With high levels of willpower you are much less likely to give in to distractions. With motivation and willpower you will find it much easier to start something and to see it through to completion. So, which category do you fall into?

i. I work hard and play hard, but work comes first.

ii. I can play any old time.

iii. Okay, I admit it, I get far too easily distracted.

iv. I really hate it when people interrupt me when I'm working.

v. It's no problem if I don't finish it today, I can always do it tomorrow.

Can You Take Responsibility?

It's far too easy to say that I'll do it tomorrow, and of course, tomorrow never comes. Now I realize that you might have perfectly legitimate reasons for not getting stuck in, after all you have more going on in life than one project or task. However, the problems kick in when you come up with reasons that are not valid. Which is easy to say but what reasons are valid? And if you have a problem with procrastination then the odds are that you will view your excuses as valid reasons.

So if you have started to procrastinate then you have to know the reasons why? And you have to identify the root cause of why you are doing so! And I am aware that the reasons and the root cause can be the same thing, but it's not always the case.

It could be the case that deep down you really don't want to do a certain project or a task, if that's the case then why? What is it about this task that so repels you? If you know the reasons why you have a problem then you can take action to deal with them. And don't forget, if this task can help you to achieve your goals, then miserable enough as the task might be, completing it will take you one step closer to achieving your goals, and that can be a powerful motivator.

Is it the case that you doubt your abilities, don't you think that you're not up to the job. Is that a genuine assessment of your talents, or is this your procrastination talking?

In order to move forward and create some forward momentum, you have to understand what the problem is that is holding you back! Until you can understand what's holding you back from starting or completing tasks, you will be unable to move forward.

The longer that it takes to deal with your problems the more difficult they will be to resolve. Once your mind becomes conditioned to deal with a certain way of thinking it can be difficult to change it, especially if that way of thinking is a negative one. If you are unable to deal with your problems then they will only get worse. It's up to you to make the necessary changes, and once you know what you are dealing with then you can come up with a course of action to deal with it.

Regardless of what problems you have, you are going to take responsibility for your task. It's your task, your responsibility. If you're having problems with your task then get help, but like it or not you will have to complete your task. If you don't accept responsibility for your task then will you get it done? You need to accept it, deal with it, and then move on to the next task, if you don't then you will achieve nothing, apart from wasting your precious time and not achieving your goals.

Does the Thought of Failure Scare You?

To be human is to fail. Things happen that are out of our control, and there is nothing that we can do about them. The only time that you can justifiably feel unhappy due to failure, is if you failed to plan to succeed. Failure is just something that shows you what doesn't work. Once you know what doesn't work, then identify what does work.

The fear of failure can be a terrible thing. It can be so powerful that for some it can paralyze their ability to move forward. At some point we all fail, nobody wants to fail in what they do but it happens, that's life, the important thing is that you learn from what has happened and then move forward. If you let your fear of failure consume you then it can disrupt your productivity, your time management, and it can even disrupt your relationships. You should always try to work to the highest possible standard, just don't set the bar too high.

When you start a project or a new task you decide what you need to achieve. If you set yourself realistic goals then the odds are that you will achieve them. Having drive and ambition is all very laudable, but if in your quest for glory you set the bar unrealistically high then you are going to really struggle to achieve your goals, and there is every chance that you will not achieve them. If you set unrealistic goals and you fail to achieve them, then you will start to question yourself. Once you start to question yourself then self-esteem start to wither. Repeated failure can bring you to the point where you just don't want to try anymore.

Fear of failure isn't always a bad thing. It can show you what doesn't work. It can teach you the best approach to a problem. The fear of failure can also drive and motivate you.

Look at sports teams, no one wants to lose so they give their all. Not everyone wins, sometimes they draw, and sometimes you lose. It's a fact of life that not everything goes according to plan. The most successful people in the world have made mistakes, but they've learned from them, and they've moved forward as stronger individuals.

The only time that you should ever take failure seriously, is if you take it seriously. When you don't think about failure you can focus on the task in hand. You have a job to do so go and do it. You can't predict or control the future so if something goes wrong, it goes wrong. Learn from it and move on.

I need you to answer often, sometimes or never to the following questions:

i.   Do you accept that at some point everyone experiences failure?

ii. If something goes wrong do you remain positive and forward looking?

iii. If something goes wrong do you network to find out what happened?

iv. Do you stand by whatever decision was made?

v. Do you try to learn from what went wrong?

vi. Do you keep allies close to you so that you can win in the future?

If you answered predominantly with often or sometimes then you show yourself as someone who finds it easier to cope with failure. If something doesn't go as you had planned then it's only natural to be unhappy, just so long as you don't take it to extremes.

If you live and die by every mistake that you make then you will have a miserable existence and you will grind yourself into the ground.

Prioritization & Time Management

Have you noticed how we all seem to be leading such busy lives, and that there never seems to be enough time to get everything done? There are times when you can look at something and go, "oh woe is me," I don't have the time to do this, so having convinced yourself that you don't have the time, you don't even start.

But what if you did have the time, but you just don't realize it?

Okay, I realize that you are busy, but if you took a moment to analyse how you prioritized your tasks, and how allocated your time, and then you just might find that you had the time.

Sometimes we can blind ourselves to just how much we are capable of doing. If we are not careful we can fill up our time with minutiae. By concentrating on the minutiae we can convince ourselves that we are getting so much work done. It's just a pity that our heroic workload isn't getting us anywhere.

Have a go at the following questions so that you can get an idea of your time management skills. Don't worry too much about your answers because these are skills that you can learn:

i. Do you with a project by getting stuck into the easy or the difficult tasks?

ii. This is important, do you have a, to do list?

iii. Are there times that you will say no when someone asks you to do something?

iv. Do you prioritize your tasks and with them in that order?

v. Do you allow a lot of introductions?

vi. Are you able to delegate or do you have to do it all yourself?

Please remember that when you are planning something, don't complicate it any more than is necessary! Try to complete your task or project in the easiest and simplest way possible! And if you need help don't be too embarrassed to ask for it, there are times when you can't do it all yourself!

Your Assertiveness

Now you need to start looking at where your strengths lie. To start with, I need you to make a list of where you think your talents lie, and what are you good at? It can also be a good idea if you can get someone who knows you to a write a list of the areas they perceive your talents to lie in. Next I need you to come up with a list of all your positive qualities. It's the combined results that will assist you in determining your strengths.

Assertiveness and Influencing Others

How you assert yourself in your interaction with others can have a bearing on how much you procrastinate. Your assertiveness and how you interact with others also has an effect on how you initiate and deal with tasks. For example if you approach a task positively and take control of it, then you are unlikely to procrastinate, whereas if you approach a task negatively and with less confidence you are much more likely to procrastinate.

The following questions have been designed to help you assess your assertiveness in 4 key areas namely whilst at work, when you're in public, when you're with friends, and when you're at home:

i. How do you react when faced with a critical individual from within the ranks of your management?

ii. How do you respond when you see that someone has made an extra effort at work, or if they've done a good job? Do you praise them or are you indifferent to them?

iii. Once in a while you might need to make comment on the lack of professionalism from a colleague or a member of staff. How do you react in those situations, are you decisive or do you struggle to criticize?

iv. Let's say that you're in a shop, and you're ready to spend your hard earned money in that shop, how do you react when the shop assistant ignores you?

v. This has probably happened to most of us. You're watching a movie and there's some kind and thoughtful person who just can't stop talking. How do you react to that individual?

vi. There are some people who only seem to come alive when they are complaining about something or someone. How would you react to a friend who used you as their audience to moan to?

vii. Let's say that you were kind enough to lend a friend some money, you now need it back but unfortunately they are being just a wee bit slow in repaying you. How would you react to them?

viii. How do you react when you are at the receiving end of moans, complaints and general trolling?

ix. How do you react when one or both of your parents are critical of you?

x. And finally, how do you react when everyone thoughtfully leaves all the housework to you?

Okay my friend. Just take a moment and think on how you would react to those situations. Are you positive, negative or in between? Use the following questions to help organize your thoughts.

i. What do you say and do, do you think before you speak or are your responses automatic?

ii. How does this kind of behavior affect you?

iii. What is the positive side of any response that you make?

iv. Conversely, what is the negative side to your response?

v. Are there any potential negative effects to your being more assertive?

Being assertive is nothing to do with aggression, it's about being very clear what you want, and then asking for it. Be sensible about what you what, but also be prepared to stand up for yourself.

If you're a manager you have to say what needs to be done and have your team respond to you. If you're standing up for your rights then you have to be firm but not inflexible. Always be prepared to talk things through, you might end up with a more workable solution. Always be prepared to compromise, you might not be able to get exactly what you want, but you might get something more realistic. And at all times make sure that you remain focused on achieving your goals.

Okay my friend. Just take a moment and think on how you would react to those situations. Are you positive, it's great that you want to take on and beat your procrastination, but in order to do so you will have to make some changes. However, you can't make those changes until you know where your problem areas are. Once you become actually aware of the skills that you have, and your character strengths then you have taken the first steps in strengthening the unique individual that you are. So take an honest look at how you answered those questions, and think on the answers that they give you.

Please don't forget that in dealing with procrastination you cannot just focus on dealing with your weaknesses, your strengths are just as important if not more so, because your strengths give you the starting point to begin your fight back, and you can use and develop your strengths to help you to move forward as an individual. So stand up for who you are and stand up for what you want to achieve.

In order to beat your procrastination, you are going to have to deal with certain facets of yourself, the first being your self-esteem.

Your Self-Esteem

Procrastination is not just about you putting off a task for as long as you are humanly able, there is more to it than that. Given that you know that you're wasting your time by procrastinating there has to be something in you that is holding you back, and until you can deal with this anchor that has you held in place, then you will not move forward. Once you can start to deal with whatever is holding you back then you can get to work on demolishing your procrastination.

So, just what is self-esteem? That could probably be the subject of a book in its own right. Self-esteem comes in at various levels, and whether you have a high or a low self-esteem very much depends on your experiences of life. Your self-esteem is that bit within you that can accept you for who you are, warts and all. You know and accept everything that makes you the unique individual that you are. You know that you've got your strengths and weaknesses, you know that being human you make mistakes, but irrespective of everything you accept yourself, although whether or not you like who you are very much depends on whether or not you have high or low self-esteem.

The first thing that you need to deal with is your self-esteem. It can be all too easy to slip into the trap of thinking that you're no good, that you're worthless, so why bother. If you are struggling with your self-esteem then it's vital that you deal with it, because by feeding your mind negative thoughts and images you can end up wallowing in self-pity and despair. The mind is a powerful thing and can make or break you. Don't ever forget that you can also feed your mind positive images and that can raise you up and positively charge your mind.

No matter who you are or what you do, you will always come across stumbling blocks in life. No matter how well you plan something, you'll be lucky if you don't have at least a few niggles along the way. But that's life, when you come up against an obstacle you deal with it, and having dealt with it you move forward. Every time that you deal with an obstacle your self-esteem gets a boost, you are showing yourself that despite everything you can succeed and that you can see your task through to the end. The more you deal with the more resilient you become, and the more your belief grows in yourself and in what you can accomplish.

Something else that can have a major effect on our self-esteem is how we are viewed by other people such as friends, family, and work colleagues. How others see us, and how they respond to us can make or break us, because unless you are a complete loner who cares about nothing or no one, then you at least appreciate the approbation of your peers, there is something in all of us, no matter how deeply it's buried that wants and needs the acknowledgment and acceptance of those around us. And it's really great if those around us are caring and supportive people, however the reality of life is that there are some miserable, malodorous individuals out there who can be somewhat negative towards you. So whilst receiving the acclaim of your peers is fantabulous, you need to become more reliant on your inner self-esteem, rather than focusing over much on the self-esteem that you gather in from your environment.

Right my friend. In order to help you to grow your inner self-esteem, you have to be able to develop an awareness about your thoughts and emotions, and then take action based on that awareness. Here are some questions for you to think on. Be brutally honest with yourself here:

i. What do you do that is centred on the need for approval from others?

ii. In order for you to feel accepted, is there anyone that you gravitate towards for approval?

iii. What personal standards have you set for yourself? So, what do you need to do in your daily life in order to win your own personal approval and to be happy with yourself?

iv. Do you find that there is conflict between your need for approval from others, and doing what it is that you want to do?

The answers that you have pulled out from your self should give you an insight into yourself, and that realization should help you to strengthen your inner self-esteem and to decrease your reliance on the need for approval from others.

Having looked at who you are, and hopefully come to some kind of understanding with your self, now it's time to start taking positive action so that you can strengthen your self-esteem and start to rid yourself of your tendency to procrastinate. The following actions will set you on the path to not only develop your self-esteem, but they will develop and strengthen you as an individual:

i. My apologies, this a bit basic I know, but it can be easy to forget. You need to become more aware of your personal growth and development.

ii. Start to take the initiative more. Don't be content to let others lead the way, show people that you can take action.

iii. You need to practice being more assertive. This is where you remind yourself that you can achieve, that you can get things done, and that you don't have to wait to be told what to do.

iv. The human mind can be such a wonderful thing, unfortunately it can also whisper sweet nothings of negativity to you. If your mind is being negative then talk back to it, tell yourself that there is more to you than your mind has let you believe, and shout down the negativity with positivity.

v. You have to set yourself goals, you need something that you can work towards that will help to move your life forward. Break down your goals into achievable steps and then move forward one step at a time. If you are always looking and working towards the future then you have direction and purpose, and you're no longer drifting aimlessly.

vi. You need to look after yourself and that includes taking care of your mind and body. It sounds a bit of a cliché but eat properly, exercise, have some fun, and don't forget to relax as well.

There is one thing that I need to say before moving on to the next section. If you ever hope to achieve the life that you want and that you deserve, then you have to build your self-esteem. If you don't have a strong, positive self-esteem then where will you get your drive, your ambition, your energy, your enthusiasm, your zest for life. Your self-esteem might be low at the moment, but you have it in you to change that, you just have to take action.

Dealing with Your Inner Negativity

Research has been shown that the majority of our daily thoughts are negative. If you're already struggling with low self-esteem, then constantly brooding on negative thoughts will make it extremely difficult to regain your positivity. The problem is that much of our negative thinking is directed towards ourselves. This is thanks in part to the environment that we live in, and the accumulation of our personal life experiences. The problem gets worse when we find ourselves faced with seemingly insurmountable obstacles. One you reach that stage a low self-esteem will eat away at your confidence, and leave you struggling to attempt move forward in a positive manner. You can deal with this negativity and beat it, it's just that you don't realize it, yet.

I don't know about yourselves, but I've lambasted myself with similar, and perhaps slightly stronger statements before. Do any of them sound familiar to you?

"That was a stupid thing to do!"
"I'm stupid, I'm lazy, I'm useless, etc, etc, etc.."
"There is no way that I'm going to be able to do this, it's far too difficult!"
"I need to do this, I have to this, there's no way that I can't do this."
"Everything depends on me getting this right!"

Can you see what all this drivel is doing to you? It's putting pressure on you that you just don't need! And the pressure that you put on yourself is infinitely worse than anything that anyone else could put you under! If you continue to let your mind have a free rein with you, then it will grind you down and you will be unable to move forward.

You have to be able to say that enough is enough and start to fight back! Your first step forward is to become consciously aware of all the negativity that your mind is feeding you, and you have to recognize it as pointless, meaningless, worthless drivel! You have to believe that you are not that person, and be aware that you are much better than that.

Your fears can talk you out of taking action. Your fears can talk you out of having ambition. That voice inside your head does not have your best interests at heart! You might not even be aware that you have a problem. In order that you can achieve your potential, you have to take action to deal with this, and get your life moving forward.

Once you can admit to yourself that you have a problem, then you need to start dealing with your negative thinking. And before you say anything, yes I do know that it's easier said than done. In order to counter your negative thoughts you have to start feeding yourself more positive affirmations.

I'm assuming that like me you are a mere mortal, so it's okay to make mistakes! It's quite natural not to get it right all the time! So don't worry about it!

Mistakes can give you the opportunity to learn, and they can give you a benchmark from which to grow. Take a look at successful people. They didn't get to where they were by not making mistakes. They learned what they could from their mistakes, and then they move forward.

Let's say that you're doing something new, maybe for the first time. Something goes wrong with whatever it is. Does that mean that you're beyond hope? Of course it doesn't! All of life is a learning process, and if you're doing something new then how can you expect to be perfect? You should be appreciative of the fact that you are trying something new, because it's by learning that we grow as individuals.

You might have an ambitious project that's staring you in the face. Does the prospect of having to tackle this behemoth scare you? It shouldn't as all you have to do is to break the project down into simple steps, and then you can complete your behemoth of a project one step at a time. By tackling everything one step at a time you will not stress your mind out at the prospect of your gargantuan goal. By taking it one step at a time you will slowly build your confidence levels and grow your self-esteem.

We all know that no matter how carefully and meticulously you plan something out, the odds favor something happening that will snarl up your plans. Will the world come to an end just because everything's not going according to schedule? Of course it won't, all you have to do is to be flexible in your planning so that if one way doesn't work, then you find another.

Now if you had given in to negative thinking, you would struggle to make any forward progress in what you're doing. I know that it sounds as if I'm over simplifying things, but if a problem occurs don't think about it, just deal with it. Over the years, and despite having more than just cause, I have learned that there is no point in giving in to that niggling voice in your head that keeps telling you that you can't do it.

The fact of the matter is that you can achieve, you can get things done, and it's just that for a while you've forgotten how capable you are.

Now I want you to start reinforcing your self-esteem, with a steady stream of positive thoughts that are all about you. Go back to that list of your strengths and positive qualities that you wrote down earlier. The next time that your mind is talking you down, then start repeating all those positive things about you. This positive reinforcement of things that you know to be true will give you a boost and make you feel positive about yourself. The more times that you affirm your positive qualities the more you will come to believe in them and in you.

Given that repetition will be the key to your success you don't have to be reactive to your negativity, be proactive. Keep topping your mind up with positive affirmations throughout the day. Look in a mirror at least once a day and tell yourself that, "**I AM GREAT**," 5 times. And remember not to think the words, but say them out **LOUD**! And when you say those words, learn to believe them.

Our negativity is in some respects like a self-defence mechanism. It tries to steer you away from things that you're uncomfortable with, and with taking risks. You can let your mind shelter you from having to take action, leap outside of your comfort zone, and succeed. If you want to get the most out of your life, then you have to be ready to take on everything and anything, and that's not going to happen if you are wallowing in negative small talk.

I think that the worst thing for those that try to hide away from their fears is that most fears never achieve any substance. If any of your fears do try to take a pop at you, then they can be dealt with, even more so when you have built up your strengths.

Fear is an intensely powerful emotion which if left unchecked can paralyze you from taking any positive action. If you let your fears rule you, then they will likely cause you to procrastinate in all areas of your life.

No matter how seemingly confident an individual is, the chances are that they have some kind of fear, it's just that some people manage their fears rather than let their fears manage them. Take a look at these strategies for managing your fears:

i. Start off by taking some small risks, don't try anything dramatic, and just take a few risks that you can feel comfortable with. And once you've done that, hold onto how good you felt when you did what you set out to do.

ii. You might feel a bit uncomfortable about this, but it can be a good idea to talk to people that you trust about your fears. See what they make of your fears. On the off chance that there is some substance to them then you have someone there that you can talk it through with. The odds are that your fears will be groundless, or that they could be just things that had got out of control. When someone that you trust says that you have nothing to worry about, then it will be a lot easier to dismiss that fear.

iii. Let yourself feel the fear, welcome it into you, and then talk it through with yourself. The more that you actually analyze your fears, the less threatening they seem. When you confront you fears and show your mind that you won't be beaten by them, then they will lose their power to affect you.

iv. As you become more accustomed to take risks, and slowly but steadily, giving your mind time to adjust to the new reckless you, increase the size of the risks that you take. Don't rush, and don't go crazy, but steadily allow your mind become used to, and comfortable with the realization that you can take risks. By not rushing things you won't set alarm bells ringing in your mind, and you will find it much easier to this new way of living.

Regardless of who you are, it's never easy to face up to your fears and deal with them. You have two choices. You can let your fears hide you away, or you can face up to them, which will it be?

Take Hold of Your Willpower & Get Motivated

You don't need to be a rocket scientist to realize that you have to have motivation in order to kick your procrastination up the bahookie. However, motivation will only get you so far, because without willpower to keep pushing you ever onwards you'll not get as far as you should.

Think of motivation as your dream form of transport, your own private jet or whatever, that carries you forward to better things. Think of willpower as the fuel for your motivation, a fuel that powers you on to your goals and through any obstacles that you meet along the way.

I think it fair to say that if you've managed to make it this far into the book, then you certainly have willpower and motivation! You want to change things in your life, otherwise wouldn't be reading this

If you are struggling to find your willpower and motivation for whatever project that you're working on, then now sounds like a good time for you to take a short time out. If possible, you would be better served tackling projects that can help to boost your motivation and willpower. Here are some exercises that can help you to build your willpower:

i. For starters, try something new, something that you've never tried before. It doesn't matter what it is, it could even be as simple as going to work by a different route. The important is that you show yourself that you can do something different, that you can break out of your mold.

ii. Do you ever get a burning desire to say something, but no matter how desperate you are to say it you know that you should not? The answer is simple, even if people start giving you strange looks and asking you if you are alright, just don't say it.

iii. You know when you have something that you really don't want to do. Even though you know you have to do it you start to drag your feet, and you end up procrastinating big time. The solution to that is to get into the habit of doing things that you don't want to do. It's probably best not to start getting stuck into huge unlikeable projects! The way to do it is to build yourself up slowly. By going slowly you allow yourself to adapt to your new way of thinking and you discover that you can take on and complete loathsome, unpalatable tasks.

iv. Here's something radical for you to do. We all know that this is a busy world and that we can all get caught up in our own lives and what we are doing. In order to try and break out of that mindset, be nice to someone. You could do something nice for someone, or you could say something nice to someone. Once you get the hang of it people will look at you in a new way, and you will feel very good about yourself.

v. Sometimes you might have something to say that offers real value and insight into the discussion, the problem is that you feel nervous about intruding your opinions. You can probably guess what I'm going to say. If you have something useful to contribute then say it. By speaking up, people will know that you have an opinion and are much more likely to include you in the conversation, because they want to hear what you have to say. And if they like what you have to say then your self-esteem is going to get a massive boost. When you speak up you show yourself that you can take action and that you can do things that you feel uncomfortable doing.

I'm not looking for you to take huge earth shattering changes, I just want you to make small but steady changes. These exercises give you a framework to grow from. Use the exercises as a starting point. Once you start to grow your willpower and your confidence in your abilities, then start adding in your own steps that are unique to who you are and your personal situation. As your willpower grows you will come to depend more on yourself because you will know that you can follow through on a situation.

Become More Assertive

It's a fact that some people are more assertive than others. And while being and assertive individual can be a lot better than being pushed into the background, there can be a fine line between assertiveness and threatening, obnoxious, bullying, arrogance. One thing is certain, and that is if you cannot manage even a smidgeon of assertiveness then you will always struggle with procrastination.

Our own personal assertiveness has evolved through a heady mixture of our life experience, attitudes, beliefs, values, feelings, thoughts, and of course our self-esteem. This complicated mix is what determines what we will do, and how we will behave in order to get what we want. If we have something that we want to achieve then we have four paths that are open to us. I will admit that I might be just a wee bit harsh here, but hey, so long as it makes you think.

We can take a passive approach, which is basically saying that you hope for the best and you're not surprised when it doesn't happen.

We can manipulate a situation, and yes you can achieve results this way, however, I would say that being manipulative was hardly the healthiest of personality traits.

You could be aggressive and effectively steam roller everyone into thinking and acting how you want them to, essentially you would be a bully, which again is hardly a particularly attractive personality trait.

On the other hand you could be assertive. You have something that you want to achieve and you will stand up for your right to achieve it. By being assertive you still need to treat people decently (which results in their co-operation and their regard), but you have to stand up for yourself and for what you need to do.

The sad thing is that far too many of us tend to go for all of the various sub categories of assertiveness. I'm guessing that we all know that being assertive is the way to move forward, the problem is that most of us are clueless when it comes to being assertive.

The theory behind being assertive is mind blowingly simple. Without ordering or without commanding people to obey, you tell people what you need doing, and then ask for their help in achieving it. By being upfront and straightforward with people it shows that you have respect for them, it also show that you have confidence and respect for yourself. If you happen to be a manager, asking people to do something rather than demanding that they do it will win you respect, and give you a more motivated team.

Being assertive means that you have to be ready to step up to the plate, it's not always the easiest of things to do and it can leave you feeling very exposed. But if you have something that you need to get done, then being assertive is your path to success. Okay, so maybe there are circumstances that conspired to thwart you, if that happens then that's life. Regardless of the outcome, by taking positive action you will show yourself that you do not have to procrastinate, you will realize that you have willpower, and you will realize that contrary to what you used to believe, you can get things done.

So let's recap. Aggressive behavior may win you short term gains, but in the long term you will lose. Aggressive people are ultra-competitive, they don't like to lose, and when it happens they take it personally, much to the detriment of their self-esteem, when they do. Aggressive behavior will not win you friends and it will not win you respect.

Conversely, if you take on a passive approach then you are likely to struggle to achieve any success. Those with a passive nature tend to have a low self-esteem. Passive behavior tends to result in a negative outcome. Those who have a predominantly passive behavior tend to have others decide what happens to them. Rightly or wrongly those of a passive nature are not viewed as people who can contribute to the task at hand, as a result they can be left out in the cold.

Those who hover around the side lines and try to manipulate events and people also tend to have problems with low self-esteem. These are people who prefer to avoid open confrontation like the plague, they would rather manipulate from the safety of the shadows rather than risk rejection. Manipulators have very little respect for themselves, and by the nature of what they are doing they have very little respect for those that they seek to control. Admittedly manipulative behavior can get results, but at a cost.

If you need some techniques to help you become more assertive, whilst avoiding the traps of becoming either aggressive or passive, then try these. Use the ones that are best suited to your situation and see how you can change things:

i. Don't be woolly headed about what it is that you want! Have your goal clearly set in your mind, be aware of what needs to be done in order to achieve it, if you need help with it then ask people to do clearly defined tasks, if you don't need help then just do it. It is a lot easier completing a task when you have a clear goal as to what you need to do, and how you will be do it. Trying to wing a project and hope for the best will not get you anywhere, whereas if you have a plan...

ii. One of the easiest ways to learn something is through repetition. If you repeat what you need to get done, then those working with you will have a clear, unambiguous idea of what you need them to do. By repeating what people are supposed to be doing, it keeps both you and those working with you focused on your task.

iii. If you have a manipulator on your team then you just need to keep on repeating their instructions. If they have a point to make then, by all means acknowledge that point, but still keep making it clear from them what you want them to do. Don't respond to any of the manipulators tricks, just be calm and don't give them the satisfaction of becoming annoyed. By remaining calm you don't waste time and energy by getting angry with that individual, it will also keep you focused on the task in hand.

iv. If this is a team project, then you are not looking for a win for you the individual, you are looking for a team victory. Even if this is a solo project, the best way to achieve success is always by setting realistic goals that can be achieved, rather than reaching for the sky and crashing down in failure. Don't forget that things happen to ensure that the best laid plans go astray, so it's worth having a fallback position, so that if things don't go as planned, then at least you can still say that you achieved. Even if nothing works out, so long as you can walk away having learnt from your mistakes then you are still a winner. Some people find it helpful to disclose their honest feelings during the interaction. For some people this alleviates guilt and anxiety. Methinks that I've gone slightly off track here, and before I get too carried away, I'll finish off this point by saying that assertiveness is nothing to do with aggression, manipulation or being meek and mild. It's about you getting the best result for you and your team, and where necessary achieving that result through negotiation and compromise.

v. If you have any problems or issues, or if members of your team have problems then talk about it. Talking about something helps, problems are never quite as bad when someone else knows about it, it clears the air, it unites people, and it helps you to move everyone and everything forward.

It really doesn't take much for you to harness your willpower and start getting motivated, you just have to say that enough is enough, and then having made the conscious decision to change, you take action. You have much better things to do with your life if you take action, than to just have it unproductively pass you by.

Anger & Frustration Management

When things aren't going too well it's far too easy to fall prey to anger and frustration. It's understandable behavior because no one wants to have things go wrong for them, but things do go wrong, and for better or for worse and no matter where you are, some measure of anger and frustration is inevitable. Yet despite their inevitability, we still invite them in and we still pay the price for that in terms of procrastination.

If you're feeling angry and frustrated do you want to let everyone know about it? Some will, but the majority of people will hide their frustrations because you don't want to look as if you're weak, and that you're unable to cope. And because we get so good at concealing our feelings from others, we can also end up far too adept at concealing them from ourselves. Our anger can manifest itself in a variety of ways such as walking away from our tasks, or being angry to people whose only fault to be close by to you. This kind of behavior is a complete and utter waste of your time, so you need to learn to recognize these feelings, and you need to learn how to deal with them.

Once you know how to recognize and accept your anger and frustration, then you have to decide what you are going to do with it. Remembering that anger and frustration are wasted emotions, you have a number of options:

i. You can walk away from the situation, and once you have control of how you're feeling then you can return to the situation that drove you away. Having returned will you do anything about that situation, or will you just carry on with what you were doing?

ii. If one task or project is causing you so much grief then have a look to see if there is anything else that you could be doing, bearing in mind that at some point you are going to have to confront that project again. Still, at least this path is better than just walking away from the situation, and it gives you a chance to vent your frustrations on some other innocent task.

iii. The path that I hope that you take is the one where you try to deal with the problem. Whatever it is, the chances are that your problem will not go away, it'll still be there gnawing away at you until you confront it and deal with it. As problems are a fact of life just accept them, deal with them and move on.

Now I have just realized that I'm maybe being a wee bit cavalier in the way that I dismiss anger and frustration, and for those of you who are muttering that he doesn't know what he's talking about (and perhaps various slightly stronger expressions along a similar line), let me explain.

Now I've collected more than sufficient reason over the years to give in to anger and frustration, but the simple fact of the matter is that I don't. Once in a while (I'm only human) I might get annoyed for a few minutes, but that's it. I can't remember the last time that I was angry, it's certainly happened but not for years. From my perspective, I genuinely cannot see the point to giving way to something that will be a complete and utter waste of time.

When I was at College I had an essay that I had to write. It was getting just a wee bit too close to the deadline. You know, it never ceases to amaze me just how inspiration can bloom when you have a deadline that is approaching faster than the speed of light.

Anyway, I headed in to my old College and started work. These were the days when most people didn't have a computer. And if you can believe that such a time existed, the vast majority of the population didn't own a mobile phone, those were happier days.

After about 10 or 11 hours (oh how time does fly when you're having fun) I had finished and I was just about to print everything out when all the computers crashed, taking what was a really great (at least as far as I remember it was) essay with them. Did I shout, did I scream, nope, I just came back the next day and mercifully finished it. One of my friends was there and he couldn't understand why I was taking it so calmly! Take a moment to think about it.

What happened had happened, there was nothing that I could do to change the past, and so where was the point in beating myself up over it? Mind you, saying all that, I've also been described as someone who if the world came to an end, would just shrug his shoulders and carry on. I hope that I'm never put to the test, but they were probably right.

Okay, and back to the plot. Try to identify whatever it is that triggers your anger and frustration. Some people still have issues from past situations which have never been dealt with, and when a similar situation pops up then out comes the old anger and frustration.

Whenever you notice your mood starting to slip, you need to regain control before it goes too far. What you can do is to find ways of channelling hose negative feelings in such a way as to get a positive result. You could always try to have a ready store of positive thoughts and memories, so that as the negativity tries to sneak in, you could always displace it with something positive. Now as we're all unique individuals it's impossible to come up with some catch all solution, you're on your own with this one, so find solutions that are best suited to you and your environment.

Stress Management

In our fast paced environment stress can be a very real danger to you. Apart from the knock on effect to your health, stress can slow you up, hold you back, and have a massive impact on your efficiency and productivity. How many times have you heard someone exclaim that they are feeling stressed out, or that they're under too much stress? Having a busy day doesn't mean that you are having a stressful day.

A stressful day happens when you are dealing with something that is beyond your ability to cope with, and as a result, your body and mind react to it. When faced with a stressful situation our natural instinct is to pass it by, and this is the point where far too many people will just walk away from their projects. Stress is not something to be taken lightly, it can impact on both your mental and physical condition, and it can disrupt your life both at home and at work.

What are the symptoms of stress?

Given that we're all different, we all have our unique histories and perspective's, so different things affect different people in different ways. As no one can really know when stress hit's, it's important to know the symptoms so that you can deal with them if they sneak up on you.

The physical symptoms of stress are unpleasant to say the least, and it's all too easy to mistake them for something else. I hasten to add that you might not be subject to all of them, but if you do have a problem then you can expect things like indigestion, colds, muscle cramp, fatigue, nausea, heart palpitations, body aches and infections. Given the mixture of symptoms, it's easy to believe that you've some down with whatever version of the plague is lolloping around your neighborhood.

If you have problems with stress then there is likely to be a significant emotional component to your symptoms. Some of the problems that you might suffer from are irritability, mood swings, tension, anxiety and a feeling of where's the point.

You could also experience behavioral symptoms. You could find that you become more prone to accidents, your performance at work could suffer, you could struggle with your concentration, you could have problems with comfort eating or not eating enough, and finally you could suffer from debilitating tiredness.

Your mind can be a powerful thing, it can be a wonderful thing, but if it's coming under stress then there are a number of symptoms that you could fall prey to. Symptoms such as having problems with your memory, indecisiveness, loss of perspective and worrying.

Hopefully you will never experience any problems, but the possibility is there, so learn what the symptoms are, because the sooner you realize that they are happening to you, the better it is for your health.

What are the Causes of Stress?

If you are aware of the various stress triggers then, should you find yourself in a high stressful situation you will be ready for them. Not everyone reacts the same way to the stressors as people deal with pressure in different ways. There are four different types of stressors and stress can come from any one stressor, or a combination of them.

i. Situational Stressors. These as the name suggests are stressors related to exceptional situations in your daily life. These cover situations such as bad news, heavy workload, the unexpected, change, and negative environmental factors. We can all get comfortable in our day-to-day routines and when something different happens, the stress can start creeping in.

ii. Life events stressors. Things happen in life, and if these things are negative then they will take us out of our comfort zone and cause us stress. By life events I'm talking about health, death, divorce, moving home, death, financial difficulties (a major problem today) and becoming parents. These are all major landmarks in our lives and they can take some getting used to, eventually (no matter how impossible it may seem at the time) you will adjust to these situations and your stress levels will drop.

iii. Stressors caused by others. These stressors can afflict you both at home and at work. The sort of problems that you can expect here are as a result of others unreasonable expectations of you, and if you have a negative atmosphere at home or at work. Sometimes people are so fixated on getting what they want that they forget the effect that it can have on others, they forget that being unreasonable can have an impact on others.

iv. And finally we have internal stressors. By and large these are stressors that we put ourselves under. Perfectionism is something that wastes more time than it's worth! You should always try to the best that you can, but lusting for perfectionism means that you'll never be satisfied, you'll never be happy with the results that you achieve, all because you don't have reasonable expectations of yourself.

By having unreasonable expectations of ourselves we are trying to be someone that we are not. If we have unreasonable expectations, then the chances are that we will not live up to those expectations. And when we don't meet our expectations then we are left with feelings of inadequacy.

Perfectionists love to be in control, and by being in control they seek to control everyone and everything. Perfectionists can lead a lonely existence where they struggle for acceptance and love.

If you don't recognize the onset of stress or that you are heading into dangerous waters, then you can end up with both physical and mental issues. It can be far too easy to slip into a stress related condition without even realizing it. Once you have a stress related problem the only way of dealing with it is if someone see's that you have a problem, because unless you know the symptoms, you are unlike to recognize that you have a problem.

Once you are aware that something is not right then you have to admit that you have a problem. And once you admit that you have a problem you have to want to take action to deal with it. You need to learn the signs so that you can deal with it. By recognizing that you have stress you are admitting that you have a problem, and once you admit to yourself that you have a problem then you need to interrupt the pattern. So that you can recognize the stress in your life you need to ask yourself the following questions:

i. What's causing your stress? Are there any triggers that you can identify in your life?

ii. When does your stress occur? Is there any particular time when you are more prone to stress?

iii. Is there a particular location where you are more likely to feel under stress?

iv. What symptoms of stress, if any are you showing?

v. Why are you reacting in this way?

vi. What can you do to decrease the levels of stress that you situation is causing you?

I suspect that far too many people won't accept that they have stress because they will be perceived as weak. Personally I believe that those who don't tackle a problem that anyone could suffer from are weak. Please don't waste your time by not acknowledging the symptoms that you are suffering, accept them and accept the fact that you now have to take action.

No one can tell you what to do, no one can make you take action, only you can do what's needed to deal with your symptoms. You have to take responsibility for you own state of being, and you have to want to take the necessary actions to deal with your symptoms.

In order to deal with you stress you need to take a bit of a time out, chill out and relax, give yourself some you time. It is a lot easier to deal with problems if you can talk it through with someone. For whatever reason it seems to be that the act of talking about your problems manages to lessen them, and they never seem quite as bad as when they were just bottled up in your mind. Now you could try to do it all yourself but there is no guarantee that you'll be successful, so why not talk things through with your close friends or family, if you have a serious problem then talk to your Doctor. It can make a massive difference to your state of mind when you know that there are people on your side.

Before you can deal with what's happening in your life you need to find what's going wrong. There will be changes that you need to make that are specific to you, but there are also some basic things that you can do to revamp your lifestyle. There are the usual healthy lifestyle changes such as eating a healthy diet and cut down on any drinking. A great way of getting some relaxation in is to exercise. Exercising can also help with mental health issues. You don't have to spend a quizzillion hours a day in the gym, you can go for walks. You might not be a big fan of exercise, but research has found that exercise can boost your self-esteem, and reduce your susceptibility to stress.

And finally if you are having negative thoughts then you have to start thinking more positively. It sounds so easy doesn't it, but it doesn't have to be all that difficult, you just have to work on your mindset. I could go on about how you should have more positive images all keyed up and ready to replace the negative images in your mind, but I won't. Instead I'll recommend what works for me.

If I'm having any negativity, I can deal with it by displacing it with positive images or thoughts. I walk 6 or 7 miles every day (which can be such fun in winter). And as the last thing that you need is for your mind to rot in front of the T.V, I have dramatically cut down on my T.V viewing. I've not come across anything that proves this, but it does make sense. You don't need to engage your mind when you watch the T.V, all you have to do is to sit and stare.

If you are having problems with negativity, then the time that you spend watching the T.V could be spent with you brooding and further exacerbating your negativity. By not turning on the T.V my world's has not come to an end, and I've plenty more mentally stimulating things that I can be doing. And as I don't vegetate in front of the T.V, I am able to relax more.

Planning & Organization

If you've not planned out a project before then you could be feeling a bit overwhelmed, especially if it's a big project. It's only quite natural that you might feel overwhelmed.

This feeling of being overwhelmed is a major cause of procrastination and it can bring us grinding to a halt, and on a bad day set us to running for the hills just so that we can escape that project. Fortunately, learning how to plan and organize what we do isn't rocket science. And once we get used to being organized, taking on fresh tasks is no longer a nightmarish proposition, and as a result we are less likely to procrastinate.

It doesn't matter how big your project is! For all I know you could be setting up a new division for some global conglomerate or putting up some shelves. The fact is that you can break down any project into nice humane, non-threatening bite size pieces.

Once the project is broken down into its constituent parts, then all you need to do is to decide the order in which you'll put those bite sized pieces together. I know, I know, that's making it look simple, and depending on your project there could be other factors involved, but when you break it down to basics, it really is that simple! Our problem is that we delight in making things much more complicated than is necessary.

Planning & Organization can be a difficult process for some people, so I've broken down into 5 easy steps:

i. You have to know what your goals are, otherwise how are you going to know what you need to do.
ii. Make sure that you know all the ins and outs of your project, as you will not be able to plan effectively if there are things that you do not know. As this could mean liaising with other departments, be prepared to ask questions.

iii. Know what you need in order to complete your project. Even if it's something simple, not having all your resources to hand can waste time and money.

iv. You've probably noticed that life doesn't always run according to plan, so factor in some flexibility into your plan for when your progress goes awry. Even if everything goes smoothly, remember to plan for the unexpected. You might not be able to plan for everything, but you can be prepared.

v. Make sure that you come up with the most detailed plan that you can. Spending time in the early stages factoring in what could happen could save you a lot more time in the long run, and can leave you less likely to get stressed out. Make sure that it's not a static plan, it needs flexibility to cope with all the vagaries of the future.

Once you start getting stuck into your project, you might discover that it could be a good idea to tweak things a bit. For example you could find that your team becomes more effective if you change people's roles. There might be a specific function where rather than have you all waste time, it could be more effective to bring in a specialist. Have you discovered that certain steps are no longer necessary, are you able to fine tune your plan to achieve greater efficiencies. Those were just some of the options available to you as your project progresses and you continually fine tune your plan. Remember to make sure that your plan is a living thing and that it accurately reflects the stage that you are at in your project.

This is one of those points that can be forgotten, and that is to effectively prioritize the steps in your project. I know that this might be seen as bit basic, but it never hurts to think on the basics now and again.

First and foremost are the urgent and priority tasks. These need to take priority over the more mundane tasks. This is followed by your important tasks. These are tasks that don't have the same urgency as your priority tasks, but nevertheless they're not ones that can be put off to a later date. There are some tasks that are urgent, but they don't require your personal attention so they can be delegated. And don't forget, if you're leading a team you can't do everything so learn to delegate! And last but not least you have the routine tasks which all need completing, but which because of their nature can be delegated or deferred. You just need to learn to balance things right, and if you're not sure, don't be too proud to ask for help or advice.

You can't do it all yourself and sometimes you have to ask for help or to work as part of a team. You can't know it all, and sometimes you will need people with specialist knowledge to help you. If you get the help that you need then you will complete your tasks more quickly. And most important of all you will achieve your goals more quickly.

Bringing Everything Together

Well my friend, you are now aware of all of the elements of procrastination, you have had the opportunity to identify which of the elements or combination of elements could be plaguing you, and you also have to skills whereby if you can't knock them into touch, you can at least diminish their hold on you. So let's bring it all together so that you can have a rational assessment of yourself that you can apply to your current situation, and how you can move yourself forward. So take what could be a long moment, to answer the following questions in as great a detail as possible:

1. To start off with you need to identify all of the areas in your life where you are prone to procrastination. It doesn't matter whether they occur in a work or a social setting, you have to know where to make the necessary changes. So take a moment to think about your life, are there any areas that you are unhappy with, or are there any areas that are crying out for change?

Once you have an idea of what needs changing then write it down in as great a detail as possible. Just creating a rough mental list won't do you much good.

By writing everything down you are having to really focus on your problem areas, and once you put pen to paper you are able to explore those areas in much greater detail than by just using your grey cells.

Next I need you to consider just how you can move your life forward. What kind of goals do you have, what is your vision for your future? You can make this your personal mission statement. Write it all down in as much detail as possible, really look at where you are now and come up with a realistic picture of where you want to be in the future. And once you have your vision for the future, work out how you are going to achieve it.

Don't forget that the way to achieve positive change in your life is through your dissatisfaction with your current situation, your vision for the future, that all important plan that will carry you forward, and most important of all, the step without which everything else is just hot air, you have to take action.

2. Now that your grey cells are focused on moving you forward, I want you to set yourself some challenges. I need you to write down each of the changes that you want to make in your life, but preface them with, "I will..." I want you to really look at everything that you want to change and ask yourself the following questions:

i. What happens if I don't bother making the changes and just leave things the way that they are?

ii. What are the consequences of being unwilling or of being unable to change?

iii. Now that I am aware of the consequences of not changing, what are the benefits of changing?

iv. Will there be any negative effects to deal with when I make the change?

v. Hopefully there will be no negative effects, but if there are, can I handle them?

Having decided on all of your changes, don't forget to make a plan on how you are going to deal with them, and don't forget to prioritize them! After all, there is no point in going through all of this work if you don't deal with the most important changes first.

3. Right, fantastic, you have set your sights on certain life changing challenges, the next step is to turn those challenges into goals. Got a pen and paper ready? Your first step is to decide a timetable for your goals, you want to have it set in your mind the point when you want to have achieved your goals by. Don't forget to factor in some flexibility here, because life just loves to make things character building for us.

Give these goals substance by writing them down on a calendar, in a journal (you could chart your progress), on your computer, or whatever suits you best. If you're really being brave you could add some accountability to your goals by telling friends and family all about them.

4. How are you going to decide if you have been successful in achieving your goals? You are going to need to come up with some criteria that quantify your success. Admittedly you could get someone else to formulate the criteria for your goals, but would that really mean anything? It's much better to set the criteria that you would use to determine success, so that once you have achieved it you will know inside yourself that you have succeeded. And as ever don't forget to write it all down.

5. When you write down your goals, leave a space below each one. The odds are that each of those goals will require you to overcome some obstacles. You should have already at least devoted some thought as to how you are going to deal with any obstacles. Beneath each write down how you are going to deal with any obstacles. Doing this also helps you to plan ahead and to be ready for any problems.

6. Once you know what you want to achieve it's time to break your goal/project down to its component steps. You can plan each individual step or plan it by sections, whatever is easiest for you.

To start with just concentrate on getting down your first 3 or 4 steps. Once you have established those steps, examine them closely. Look at the positives and negatives for each, and refine them where necessary so that what you end up with are the optimal steps.

7. The final step is to rinse and repeat the process. Don't settle for any step until you have weighed up the pros and cons. Make sure that you factor some degree of flexibility into your plan for those fun days when nothing wants to go right.

Please remember that there is no shame in modifying your plan! Your plan should be a living plan that best reflects your current position and how you can achieve your goals from that position. Whenever you look at your plan you should be able to tell where you are at that point in time.

Just a few more quick thoughts for when working on your projects, all pretty standard stuff, but as ever, it never hurts to refresh the old grey cells. Monitor and review your goals and projects just in case things are going awry. In order to focus your mind, begin by asking yourself the following questions:

i. Overall how is your project progressing, look at what has gone right and what's not gone according to plan?

ii. Given everything that's happened and could still happen, are you still on track to complete your goal according to the success criteria that you have set yourself?

iii. If things aren't quite going to plan are there any changes that you could make in order to keep everything on track?

iv. Again, given what's happened and what still could happen, is there anything new that you could add to your plan in order to stay on track, or is it a case of refine and perfect what you already have?

v. Do you need to bring in any extra help in order to complete your project? Please remember that asking for help is not a sign of weakness, it's a recognition that you can't do it all yourself, and it's the acceptance that you need to make the best use of your available resources if you want to complete your project.

8. Take a long look at yourself to see if you're already making use of the skills that you've learned in this book. I'm going to be cruel and say be honest with yourself on how well you use these skills, and be even more honest with yourself about your strengths and weaknesses. Don't forget to write everything down. As well as helping to focus your thoughts more, having a written record is also useful as a template for any future project.

9. This one is easily forgotten and that's to look after yourself! Healthy body, healthy mind! Make sure that you eat properly, get some exercise in, practice some stress relieving techniques, and don't forget to treat yourself once in a while. Life can be dreich and drear if you don't treat yourself to some pleasures in life Treating yourself is also a great way to reward yourself for doing well, and can be a great motivator.

10. As you get close to the finish line for your project, take a bit of a time out so that you can evaluate what you have achieved, and here I'm not looking at how successful your project has been, I want you to think on how you have changed as a person. Take a look at your goals, are you on target or are you not quite there yet? By now I hope that you've realized that you can beat procrastination.

So what areas of procrastination have you been able to beat? Do you have any problem areas that you still need to work on? As ever, write it all down! Write down every single thing that you have achieved! By writing it all down you think about it, and by thinking about what you've achieved there is no way of escaping the fact that you know in yourself that you can achieve.

So finally the big day has arrived and you have crossed the finish line with your project. So celebrate, enjoy yourself, have fun. It doesn't matter if you didn't meet all your goals along the way, the important thing is that you've completed your project, and you've shown that you can beat procrastination. You have the skills to beat procrastination, now it's just up to you to go and do it!

If you've managed to make it this far then you have everything that you need to beat procrastination, so take action and do something about it! Please don't let this be one of those books that you read, absorb and do nothing with what you learn! You just need to want to take those steps to become a more positive and assertive individual, and you need to take action on that want!

Notes